SpringerBriefs in Law

More information about this series at http://www.springer.com/series/10164

Rossana Deplano

The Strategic Use of International Law by the United Nations Security Council

An Empirical Study

Springer

Rossana Deplano
Brunel Law School
Brunel University London
Uxbridge
UK

ISSN 2192-855X ISSN 2192-8568 (electronic)
SpringerBriefs in Law
ISBN 978-3-319-21280-7 ISBN 978-3-319-21281-4 (eBook)
DOI 10.1007/978-3-319-21281-4

Library of Congress Control Number: 2015943795

Springer Cham Heidelberg New York Dordrecht London

Printed on acid-free paper

Springer International Publishing AG Switzerland is part of Springer Science+Business Media (www.springer.com)

To Nara and Paolo

Contents

Abstract

This book examines the strategic use of international law by the United Nations Security Council. It offers insights on whether international law is able to shape the politics of the Security Council and the extent to which the latter contribute to the development of international law. By providing a systematic analysis of the quantity and quality of international legal instruments referred to in the text of resolutions, the book reconstructs patterns of Security Council's behavioural regularities and assesses them against the provisions of the United Nations Charter establishing its mandate. The analysis is divided into three periods—origins and cold war period, post-cold war period and the twenty-first century, where resolutions are assessed by thematic categories. The book argues that while international law plays an important role in shaping the politics of the Security Council, the Security Council resolutions do not contribute significantly to the development of international law.

Chapter 1
Introduction

1.1 The Security Council as Global Actor

The study of the laws governing the functioning of the United Nations Security Council (SC) has fascinated generations of scholars from various fields, including international relations, history and law. From international legal perspective, the main point of attraction is represented by the powers bestowed on the SC by the founders of the UN Charter. Such powers are both legal, as long as they have been enshrined in the UN Charter, and highly discretional, since they are not subject to the formal scrutiny and control of any international subject other than the SC itself.

The history of the United Nations shows that the SC has acquired a special status in the international plane as one of the principal bodies of a quasi-universal international organization and, at the same time, as a global actor on its own. This has generated a growing concern among the international community about the legitimacy of SC actions. Hence, demands for reforming the SC started to be raised in 1955, when the process of decolonization led to a significant increase in the UN membership.[1] Since then, proposals for reform have focused on three main domains—namely, the issue of composition of the SC, the issue of veto power and the issue of transparency of its decision-making process.

As of today, the issue of reform of the SC remains one of the great constitutional challenges of UN law. Indeed, although proposals for reform presented over the years have been mainly motivated by political reasons, they have inspired a wealth of scholarly contributions on this topic.[2] The academic debate proves to be particularly variegated as different contributions draw upon different conceptions of both the role of the United Nations in global politics and the role of the SC as a global actor. For instance, the United Nations has been referred to either as a tool of Great Powers, a vision according to which the UN is a creature of the world's

[1]Bourandonis (2005), p. 14.
[2]See, among many, Hassler (2013); Malone (2008), pp. 131–132; Weiss and Karen (2005), pp. 131–154; Fassbender (2004), pp. 341–356.

R. Deplano, *The Strategic Use of International Law by the United Nations Security Council*, SpringerBriefs in Law, DOI 10.1007/978-3-319-21281-4_1

strongest states, or as governor of society of states, a conception of the United Nations as the guardian of an agreed-upon set of norms and values, namely the one embedded in its constitutive Charter.[3] The majority of contributions on the role of the SC, on the other hand, characterize it as the world government and point out the risk of it growing into a Leviathan.[4] The main signals of this potential—or, for some, actual—authoritarian drift pertain to the current SC composition and decision-making procedures, including the existence of veto powers.

A common trait of all academic contributions is that they recognise that in order to be effective in the international plane, the United Nations has been created with a necessary element of power to be shared by member states through the work of its main organs.[5] The division of power, however, has been unequal among member states and primary bodies alike, as the provisions of the UN Charter establishing the SC demonstrate. Acknowledging this fact, international scholars have often characterized the legal status of the SC as problematic and have called for SC reform.

From this perspective, the debate about reforming the SC can also be qualified as a discourse about taming global power. It therefore represents an issue of global constitutionalism, since the latter concerns itself profoundly with allocation of power and institutional efficacy.[6] In part, the history of the debate about SC reform reflects this standing so long as states have never really questioned the existence of permanent members, but rather who should be regarded as a Great Power.[7] Accordingly, some argue that the composition of the SC should reflect the democratic representation of the wider UN membership, while others maintain that the composition of the SC should represent global powers.[8] However, both in theory and in practice, it is difficult to determine which position better serves the purposes and principles of the UN Charter and whether it is necessary to have a democratic SC in order to maintain international peace and security.[9]

1.2 Background of Research and Aim of Study

Scholarly literature on the mandate and the powers of the SC has examined various aspects of the functions of the SC stemming from Article 24 of the UN Charter and how they relate to general international law.[10] Certain scholars also argue that the

[3]Barnett and Finnemore (2008), pp. 43–48; Chesterman et al. (2008), p. 583.

[4]Hassler (2013), p. 2.

[5]Chesterman et al. (2008), p. 19; Schweigman (2001), pp. 288–289; Hassler (2013), p. 2.

[6]Franck (2009), p. xiv.

[7]Hassler (2013), pp. 5, 220 and 232.

[8]See UN Charter Art. 23(1) on equitable geographical distribution.

[9]Hassler (2013), p. 3 (stressing that "Few… consider the question whether it is reform that should be aimed for, or whether better use should be made of the Council in its present form").

[10]See, in general, Delbrück (2002), p. 442.

SC has gradually developed its legislative competencies beyond the text of the UN Charter and probably in violation of international law.[11] Consequently, other scholars have proposed different approaches to what they perceive as a necessary curtailment of SC enforcement powers.[12]

The contribution of such a body of literature to the rationalization of principles of law governing the functioning of the Council is highly relevant. However, SC practice has never been analysed in a systematic way, with the consequence that, as of today, we do not have a comprehensive picture of the extent to which, if any, the often advocated rules of international law are able to constrain the discretionary powers of the SC.

Existent scholarship provides an account of the legitimacy of SC actions (and inactions) from a theoretical perspective using selected resolutions as case-studies.[13] Such a vast body of literature has covered various fields, ranging from the limits of the SC mandate to its lawmaking powers,[14] and has devised a number of conceptual templates whose relevance within and outside the academia cannot be underestimated. However, due to the nature of the inquiry, traditional analysis turns out to be rooted on assumptions or generalizations derived from the study of selected, though important, SC resolutions. Consequently, its findings are supported by little evidence of consolidated SC practice.

For example, it has become commonplace to argue that the decision-making at the SC is ultimately governed by reasons of political convenience.[15] The main argument put forward to support this view is that the presence of five permanent members (P5) endowed with veto power over resolutions determines that the SC mandate can be executed only when there is agreement among them.[16] As a result, situations representing actual or potential breaches of international peace and security are likely to be overlooked whenever they involve a direct interest of a P5.[17] This seems to be confirmed by the fact that, for instance, since 1946 not a single resolution has been adopted on Tibet or Chechnya while only one has been adopted in 1960 on the relationship between Cuba and the United States.[18] More recently, a draft resolution on Crimea has been vetoed by one P5, due to opposed

[11]Powell (2007), p. 157. See also Tsagourias (2011), p. 539; Rosand (2005), p. 542; Akram and Shah (2005), p. 431; Marschik (2005), p. 457. Fassbender also argues that the legislative power is jointly held by the UN General Assembly and the SC, which also exercises executive powers. See Fassbender (1998), p. 574.

[12]In a celebrated book, de Wet assessed the role of *jus cogens* and human rights norms in limiting the SC's enforcement powers, as set forth in Chap. 7 of the UN Charter. See de Wet (2004).

[13]Henderson and Lubell (2013), p. 369.

[14]See, among many, Malone (2008), p. 117; Chesterman et al. (2008); Tzanakopoulos (2013); de Wet (2004).

[15]Barnett and Finnemore (2008), p. 41.

[16]Rodley and Çalı (2010), p. 226.

[17]Rodley and Çalı (2010).

[18]Res 144(1960).

views and conflicting interests with the proponent P5.[19] However, as of today no study has ever provided a detailed list of the issues addressed in the resolutions adopted, with a view to ascertain the overall degree of legitimacy and effectiveness of such actions.

The present study aims at addressing this knowledge gap. The purpose of the research is to establish the extent to which, if any, international law is able to limit the discretionary powers of the SC, and how the behavioural patterns of the SC contribute to the creation or development of international law. In particular, this study aims to determine how international law influences the politics of the SC and how the politics of the SC contribute to the development of international law.

1.3 The Power of Numbers

One of the reasons for the existent gap in the literature can be ascribed to the limits of the traditional, doctrinal method of inquiry, which is grounded on theoretical assumptions against which selected case-studies are assessed. Thus, to pursue a systematic and comprehensive analysis of SC practice from the origins up to the present, I have adopted an empirical methodology—namely, the one that falls within the tradition of Empirical Legal Studies (ELS).[20] This is an innovative approach in international law because by using quantitative techniques, it provides new insights on how UN law actually works in practice.[21] The analysis, however, is meant to complement doctrinal scholarship on SC powers without replacing it.

Quantitative analysis depends on the language of numbers, which makes the empirical evidence particularly hard to contradict or deny.[22] Thus, the bulk of the analysis is based on simple statistics describing patterns of SC resolutions. The caution though is that ELS cannot be regarded as an end in itself, because counting for the sake of counting amounts to nothing. This means that any empirical study on law, including the present one, presupposes a background of doctrinal and normative analysis.

As an autonomous field of research, ELS possesses its own distinctive features. Generally speaking, two elements characterize the empirical research in social science. The first one is represented by the systematic nature of the process of

---

[19]Draft Res 189(2014).

[20]Epstein and Martin (2014); Kritzer (2010), p. 875; see also Kritzer (2009). On the growing demand for empirical research on law, see Epstein and King (2003), p. 311; Genn et al. (2006).

[21]UN law, like the law of the sea and the law of diplomatic protection, is virtually unexplored from an empirical perspective. On this issue, see Ginsburg and Shaffer (2010), p. 780. Other studies have analysed selected aspects of international economic law, international investment law, international criminal law and international human rights law. See, for example, Posner and de Figueredo (2005); Puig (2014); Simmons and Braidenbach (2011); Franck (2008); Fauchald (2008); Bohlander and Findlay (2002); Elkins et al. (2013).

[22]See, for instance, Crootof (2013).

collecting and analysing the information.[23] The second one consists of the rather descriptive way of presenting the results of empirical legal research, which is followed by a discussion of the implications of the empirical evidence. A corollary of the second rule is that, unlike other empirically oriented fields such as socio-legal studies and law and economics, ELS is limited to the analysis of a strictly legal issue and does not address other extra-legal concerns.[24]

To collect the information needed to conduct the empirical study of SC practice, an original database has been created. Using the descriptive formulation provided for each resolution in the SC digital archive,[25] the entire body of resolutions has been reorganized into categories—namely, resolutions on geopolitical regions, thematic resolutions and a residual category—and sub-categories. The process of coding data allows to reconstruct groups of re-cited resolutions—e.g. resolutions on Cyprus, the Middle East, threats to international peace and security caused by terrorist acts etc.—some of which span across decades of SC practice and seem to be ongoing issues on the SC agenda. The findings of this process suggest that the SC actions are tainted by selection bias, with the vast majority of resolutions addressing issues taking place in Africa and the Middle East. In order to further advance the analysis, for each of the 2,195 resolutions adopted by the SC between 1946 and 2014, the database provides information on which sources of international law—international treaties, customary international law, UN documents etc.—the SC refers to in the text of resolutions.

In order to present the data, the study is organized along two lines of inquiry. Firstly, the analysis of resolutions has been split into three periods: origins and cold war period, which is characterized by the paucity of sources of international law relied upon by the SC; post-cold war period, whose distinctive features are the increase in size of the text of individual resolutions and the practice of referring to previous SC resolutions; finally, the landmark of twenty-first century resolutions is the introduction of thematic resolutions on women, children and civilians, which establish that specific categories of state and non-state actions constitute, as a matter of principle, threats to or breaches of international peace and security and may, therefore, justify SC intervention.

Secondly, within each of the three above-mentioned periods, the resolutions addressing actual or potential breaches of international peace and security in abstract terms, rather than country-specific situations, have been singled out. Subsequent analysis and conceptualisation of such resolutions shows that four sets of thematic resolutions—namely, the thematic resolutions on women, children, civilians and international terrorism—seem to have acquired a special status in SC practice and are often referred to in resolutions addressing other subject-matters.

---

[23]Kritzer and Cane (2010), p. 4. Data collected may be either quantitative or qualitative. See Kritzer (2010), p. 883. For an overview of qualitative techniques in social science research, see Webley (2010), p. 926ff.

[24]On the intellectual origins of the ELS movement and its relation to other disciplines, see Eisenberg (2011); Heise (2002); Ho and Kramer (2013).

[25]<www.un.org/en/sc/documents/resolutions/> accessed 17 June 2015.

Here is where international law plays a particular role in shaping the politics of the SC: thematic resolutions address humanitarian concerns raised by the repercussions of military intervention on civilians, of which women and children are regarded as special categories. The text of such resolutions is rippled with references to international law, including international human rights law, international humanitarian law and refugee law, which are flagged as the legal basis of SC actions and, therefore, represent the parameter of legality of its actions. Furthermore, to the extent that the SC has decided to be bound by the principles set out in these resolutions, the latter represent neither implied powers nor *ultra vires*: they appear to be 'self-imposed duties'.

1.4 Power in Numbers

The focus of the empirical study is on resolutions, since they are generally regarded as the category of substantive SC decisions endowed with the greatest political importance.[26] The findings of the analysis show that the vast majority of SC resolutions address issues with a regional scope while nearly one fifth of resolutions include actions previously agreed upon or taken by the broader family of UN institutions and seconded by the SC. The remaining resolutions target thematic issues, such as the protection of civilians in armed conflict, children in armed conflict and the role of women in securing international peace.

Specifically, in the period from 1945 to 2014, the SC issued 2,195 resolutions. The aggregated data analysis demonstrates that 78 % of all SC resolutions address topics related to a specific geo-political area. The disaggregated data in this section further demonstrates that 743 resolutions—comprising 43 %, concern the African continent; 469 decisions—comprising 27 %, concern the Middle East region;[27] 321 resolutions—comprising 19 %, concern Europe while 182 resolutions—comprising 11 %, concern other geographical regions. Taken together, the number of SC decisions addressing issues taking place in Africa and in the Middle East is equal to 1,212 out of 1,715, comprising 70 %.

However, SC practice has not been constant over the decades. In the period of time from the origins to the cold war (1945–1991), the majority of resolutions on geo-political areas address issues taking place in the Middle East while in the post-cold war period (1991–2000) equally address issues taking place in Africa and Europe. Finally, the resolutions of the twenty-first century (2001–2014) are characterized by a sharp focus on issues taking place in Africa and a substantial development of thematic, rather than country-specific, resolutions.

---

[26]Simma et al. (2002), pp. 519–520. On the interpretation of SC resolutions, see Orakhelshvili (2007).

[27]There is no generally accepted definition of Middle East. For the purposes of this study, the broadest concept is used. See Ylmaz (2012), p. 11.

Within this context, the use of international law by the SC has gradually evolved, ranging from the quasi-inexistence during the cold war period to the development of thematic resolutions. However, the findings of the analysis suggest that while international law plays an important role in shaping the politics of the SC, the SC resolutions do not contribute significantly to the development of international law. This also suggests that the SC has developed a self-contained legal mind under the aegis of the UN Charter and that this evolutionary process poses a threat to the legitimacy of current SC practice.

The study advances existent scholarship in two ways. Firstly, it utilises an empirical, rather than doctrinal, research methodology. Consequently, for every issue analysed, theory and practice support each other and turn out to be unavoidably intertwined. Secondly, it proposes the new theory of self-imposed duties, which may redefine the very idea of international peace and security. Without the process of coding and analysing resolutions in a systematic way, it would not have been possible to single out trends of thematic resolutions and put them in context of SC practice. This bird's eye view represents, so to speak, the basis of the theory of SC self-imposed duties.

The self-contained nature of ELS entails that the empirical analysis is usually preceded by a brief overview of the normative background of research, which also makes the analysis accessible to the non-specialist reader. Thus Chap. 2 provides an overview of both the normative framework delimiting the SC mandate and the various types of SC powers. Chapter 3 provides a conceptual map of the use of international law by the SC and its variation over time. Chapter 4 provides a systematic analysis of thematic resolutions while Chap. 5 evaluates whether SC resolutions are tainted by selection bias and whether international law is able to mitigate the consequences of the charge of bias. Chapter 6 concludes.

Bibliography

Akram, Munir, and Shah, Syed H. 2005. The Legislative Powers of the United Nations Security Council. In *Towards world constitutionalism. Issues in the legal ordering of the world community*, eds. Ronald St John Macdonald and Douglas M Johnston, 431-455. Leiden: Martinus Nijhoff Publishers.

Barnett, Michael, and Martha Finnemore. 2008. Political approaches. In *The Oxford handbook on the United Nations*, ed. Thomas G. Weiss, and Sam Daws, 43–48. New York: Oxford University Press.

Bohlander, Michael, and Mark Findlay. 2002. The use of domestic sources as a basis for international criminal law principles. *The Global Community Yearbook of International Law and Jurisprudence* 2: 3–26.

Bourandonis, Dimitris. 2005. *The history and politics of UN Security Council reform*. New York: Routledge.

Chesterman, Simon, Thomas M. Franck, and David M. Malone. 2008. *Law and practice of the United Nations—documents and commentary*. New York: Oxford University Press.

Crootof, Rebecca. 2013. Constitutional convergence and customary international law. *Harvard International Law Journal Online* 54: 195–203.

de Wet, Erika. 2004. *The chapter VII powers of the United Nations Security Council*. Oxford: Hart Publishing.
Delbrück, Jost. 2002. Article 24—functions and powers. In *The Charter of the United Nations: A commentary*, ed. Bruno Simma, Vol. I, 442–452. Oxford: Oxford University Press.
Droubi, Sufyan. 2014. *Resisting United Nations Security Council resolutions*. Abingdon: Routledge.
Eisenberg, Theodore. 2011. The origins, nature, and promise of empirical legal studies and a response to concerns. *University of Illinois Law Review* 5: 1713–1738.
Elkins, Zachary, Ginsburg, Tom, and Simmons, Beth. 2013. Getting to rights: Treaty ratification, constitutional convergence, and human rights practice. *Harvard International Law Journal* 54: 61–95.
Epstein, Lee, and Andrew D. Martin. 2014. *An introduction to empirical legal research*. New York: Oxford University Press.
Epstein, Lee, and Gary King. 2003. Building an infrastructure for empirical research in the law. *Journal of Legal Education* 53: 311–320.
Fassbender, Bardo. 2004. Pressure for Security Council Reform. In *The UN Security Council: From the cold war to the 21st Century*, ed. David M. Malone, 341–356. Boulder, Colo.: Lynne Rienner.
Fassbender, Bardo. 1998. The United Nations charter as constitution of the international community. *Columbia Journal of Transnational Law* 36: 529–619.
Fauchald, Ole K. 2008. The legal reasoning of ICSID tribunals—an empirical analysis. *European Journal of International Law* 19: 301–364.
Franck, Susan D. 2008. Empiricism and international law: Insights for investment treaty dispute resolution. *Virginia Journal of International Law* 48: 767–815.
Franck, Thomas M. 2009. International Institutions: Why Constitutionalize? In *Ruling the world? Constitutionalism, international law and global governance*, ed. Jeffrey L. Dunoff and Joel P. Trachtman, xi–xiv. New York: Cambridge University Press.
Genn, Dame Hazel, Martin Partington, and Sally Wheeler. 2006. *Law in the real world: Improving our understanding of how law works. Final report and recommendations*. London: The Nuffield Foundation.
Ginsburg, Tom, and Shaffer, Gregory. 2010. How does international law work?. In *The Oxford handbook of empirical legal* research, eds. Herbert M Kritzer and Peter Cane New York: Oxford University Press.
Hassler, Sabine. 2013. *Reforming the UN Security Council membership: The illusion of representativeness*. Abingdon: Routledge.
Heise, Michael. 2002. The past, present, and future of empirical legal scholarship: Judicial decision making and the new empiricism. *University of Illinois Law Review* 4: 819–850.
Henderson, Christian, and Noam Lubell. 2013. The contemporary legal nature of UN Security Council ceasefire resolutions. *Leiden Journal of International Law* 26: 369–397.
Ho, Daniel, and Larry Kramer. 2013. Introduction: The empirical revolution in law. *Stanford Law Review* 65: 1195–1202.
Kritzer, Herbert M. 2009. Empirical legal studies before 1940: A bibliographic essay. *Journal of Empirical Legal Studies* 6: 925–968.
Kritzer, Herbert M, and Cane, Peter (2010) Introduction. In *The Oxford handbook of empirical legal research*, eds. Herbert M. Kritzer and Peter Cane, 1–7. New York: Oxford University Press.
Kritzer, Herbert M. 2010b. The (nearly) forgotten early empirical legal research. In *The Oxford handbook of empirical legal research*, ed. Herbert M. Kritzer, and Peter Cane, 875–900. New York: Oxford University Press.
Malone, David M. 2008. Security Council. In *The Oxford handbook on the United Nations*, ed. Thomas G. Weiss, and Sam Daws, 117–135. New York: Oxford University Press.
Marschik, Axel. 2005. Legislative powers of the security council. In *Towards world constitutionalism. Issues in the legal ordering of the world community*, eds. Ronald St John Macdonald and Douglas M Johnston, 457–492. Leiden: Martinus Nijhoff Publishers.

Orakhelshvili, Alexander. 2007. The acts of the Security Council: Meaning and standards of review. *Max Planck Yearbook of United Nations Law* 11: 143–195.
Posner, Eric, and Miguel F. de Figueredo. 2005. Is the International Court of Justice biased? *Journal of Legal Studies* 34: 599–630.
Powell, Cathleen. 2007. The Legal Authority of the United Nations Security Council. In *Security and human rights*, eds. Benjamin J Goold and Liora Lazarus, 157–183. Oxford: Hart Publishing.
Puig, Sergio. 2014. Social capital in the arbitration market. *European Journal of International Law* 25: 387–424.
Rodley, Nigel, and Başak Çalı. 2010. Use of force in international law. In *International law for international relations*, ed. Başak Çalı, 213–233. New York: Oxford University Press.
Rosand, Eric. 2005. The Security Council as "Global Legislator": Ultra vires or ultra innovative? *Fordham International Law Journal* 28: 542–590.
Schweigman, David. 2001. *The authority of the security council under chapter VII of the UN charter*. The Hague: Kluwer Law International.
Simma, Bruno, Stefan Brunner, and Hans-Peter Kaul. 2002. Article 27—voting. In *The Charter of the United Nations: A commentary*, ed. Bruno Simma, 476–523. Oxford: Oxford University Press.
Simmons, Beth A., and Andrew B. Braidenbach. 2011. The empirical turn in international economic law. *Minnesota Journal of International Law* 20: 198–222.
Tsagourias, Nicholas. 2011. Security Council legislation, article 2(7) of the UN Charter, and the principle of subsidiarity. *Leiden Journal of International Law* 24: 539–559.
Tzanakopoulos, Antonios. 2013. *Disobeying the security council*. Oxford: Oxford University Press.
Webley, Lisa. 2010. Qualitative approaches to empirical legal research. In *The Oxford handbook of empirical legal research*, ed. Herbert M. Kritzer, and Peter Cane, 926–950. New York: Oxford University Press.
Weiss, Thomas G., and Karen E. Young. 2005. Security Council reform? *Security Dialogue* 36: 131–154.
Ylmaz, Huseyn. 2012. The Eastern question and the Ottoman Empire. The genesis of the Near and the Middle East in the nineteenth century. In *Is there a Middle East? The evolution of a geopolitical concept*, eds. Michael E. Bonine, Abbas Amanat, and Michael E. Gasper, 11–35. Stanford: Stanford University Press.

Chapter 2
Overview of Security Council Powers

2.1 Introduction

This chapter provides a brief overview of the normative background of the Security Council (SC) powers, which represents the backdrop against which to evaluate the empirical study. The analysis is aimed at enabling even the non-specialist reader to grasp with the main elements of the system of collective security devised by the UN Charter. Thus, the review of the topic is left intentionally succinct and to a certain extent remains descriptive. However, this step is essential to appreciate the implications of the empirical analysis.

On one hand, the sections on Charter powers and implied powers address theoretical issues and, therefore, are entirely based on normative and doctrinal analysis. On the other hand, the section on the legislative powers of the SC adopts an empirical perspective and shows that, contrary to what is generally assumed, the so-called legislative powers of the SC did not originate in resolution 1373(2001) and resolution 1540(2004), but rather trace back to the cold war period. This section also shows how the use of legislative powers has evolved over the decades and problematizes the confusion generated by the language used in the text of resolutions. Examples provided include the resolutions on Southern Rhodesia and those on combating international terrorism, where the SC has at times addressed the same sort of request to 'all States', and at times to 'all Member States' or simply to 'States,' without any further specification. In these and similar situations, it is unclear whether, and to what extent, the SC is exercising legislative powers.

R. Deplano, *The Strategic Use of International Law by the United Nations Security Council*, SpringerBriefs in Law, DOI 10.1007/978-3-319-21281-4_2

2.2 Charter Powers

Article 24 of the UN Charter provides that the SC holds primary responsibility for the maintenance of international peace and security and, in discharging its duty, it acts on behalf of the UN members.[1] The same provision delimits the scope of the SC mandate.

On one hand, it establishes that the SC shall act in accordance with the four purposes and seven principles of the UN Charter.[2] According to Article 1 thereof, the purposes of the UN are: to maintain international peace and security; to develop friendly relations among nations; to achieve international cooperation; and to be a centre for harmonizing the actions of nations in the attainment of these common ends. In pursuit of the UN purposes, the SC must act in accordance with the principles set forth in Article 2 of the UN Charter. They comprise: sovereign equality of all UN members; fulfilment in good faith of the UN Charter obligations; peaceful settlement of international disputes; prohibition of threat or use of force against the territorial integrity or political independence of any state; members' assistance in any action—preventive or enforcement action—the UN takes; compliance by non-UN members with the principles of the UN Charter; and non-intervention in matters which are within the domestic jurisdiction of any state.

On the other hand, Article 24, paragraph 2, establishes that the specific powers of the SC are those laid down in Chapters VI (Pacific Settlement of Disputes), VII (Actions with Respect to Threats to Peace, Breaches of Peace and Acts of Aggression), VIII (Regional Agreements) and XII (International Trusteeship System)[3] of the UN Charter.

Chapter VI establishes that in the event of a dispute which is likely to endanger the maintenance of international peace and security, the parties to the dispute should seek a pacific solution.[4] Within this context, Article 33, paragraph 2, of the UN Charter endows the SC with the discretional power of inviting the parties to settle their dispute by pacific means. Chapter VI also provides for a role of the General Assembly in the pacific settlement of disputes. Such role, however, is subordinated to the powers of the SC in that while member or non-member states may bring to the attention of the SC or the General Assembly any dispute the continuance of which is likely to endanger the maintenance of international peace and security,[5] the proceedings of the General Assembly are subject to the provisions of Articles 11

[1]For an overview of the institutional traits of the SC, see Malone (2008), p. 117.

[2]For a short commentary, see Chesterman et al. (2008), pp. 22–24.

[3]The Trusteeship Council suspended operations on 1 November 1994, with the independence of Palau, the last UN trust territory, on 1 October 1994. See <www.un.org/en/mainbodies/trusteeship/> accessed 17 June 2015.

[4]UN Charter, Art. 33, para. 1.

[5]UN Charter, Art. 35, para. 2, of the UN Charter provides that a non-member state must be a party to the dispute and must have accepted in advance the UN Charter obligations on the pacific settlement of disputes.

and 12 of the UN Charter.[6] In addition, the SC has the power to investigate any dispute,[7] to recommend appropriate procedures or methods of adjustment[8] or such terms of settlement as it may consider appropriate.[9]

The provisions of Chapter VII regulate the use of armed forces by the SC. Measures at the disposal of the SC to prevent an aggravation of situations representing actual or potential breaches of international peace and security include recommendations and provisional measures.[10] Decisions of the SC to maintain international peace and security may also include measures not involving the use of armed force such as interruption of economic relations and of various means of communication as well as the severance of diplomatic relations.[11]

Articles 43–49 deal with SC actions involving the use of force. They establish that all UN Members undertake to make available to the SC armed forces, assistance and facilities, in order to allow it to discharge its duties.[12] The decisions of the SC must be implemented by the UN Members, either directly or through their actions in international organizations of which they are members.[13] However, the powers of the SC do not prevent individual members to act in self-defence if attacked, until the SC takes the necessary measures to maintain international peace and security.[14] On top of that, any state, member or non-member, which finds itself affected by special repercussions caused by SC intervention has the right to consult the SC to discuss a solution of those problems.[15]

Chapter VIII regulates the pacific settlement of local disputes through regional arrangements or organizations.[16] Such arrangements or organizations can be resorted to either on the initiative of states concerned or by reference from the SC,[17] provided that their activities are consistent with the purposes and principles of the

---

[6]UN Charter, Art. 33, para. 3. The General Assembly has the power to discuss any questions relating to the maintenance of international peace and security. However, questions on which action is required must be referred to the SC (Art. 11, para. 2) and when the SC is exercising its powers in relation to any dispute or situation, the General Assembly cannot make any recommendation with regard to that dispute or situation (Art. 12, para. 1).

[7]UN Charter, Art. 34.

[8]UN Charter, Art. 36, para. 1.

[9]UN Charter, Art. 37, para. 2.

[10]UN Charter Arts. 39–40. For a comprehensive analysis of Chapter VII provisions, see de Wet (2004).

[11]UN Charter, Art. 41.

[12]Details of the required cooperation with the SC must be negotiated and agreed upon in advance (Art. 43). The strategic direction of any armed forces placed at the disposal of the SC is decided with the assistance of the Military Staff Committee (Arts. 45–47).

[13]UN Charter, Art. 48.

[14]UN Charter, Art. 51.

[15]UN Charter, Art. 50.

[16]The leading publication in the field is Abass (2004).

[17]UN Charter Art. 52, para. 3.

UN Charter.[18] However, no enforcement action can be taken without the authorization of the SC.[19]

In addition to the above, Article 26 confers on the SC the responsibility for formulating plans for the establishment of a system for the regulation of armaments. The rationale behind such provision consists of arguments aimed at preserving the efficiency both of the UN and of the world's human and economic resources.

2.3 Implied Powers

The doctrine of implied powers of international organizations is widely accepted.[20] However, there is no generally accepted definition of 'implied powers'. In the *Reparation for Injuries* case the International Court of Justice (ICJ) established that:

> Under international law, the Organization must be deemed to have those powers which, though not expressly provided in the Charter, are conferred upon it by necessary implication, as being essential to the performance of its duties.[21]

In relation to specific implied powers of the SC, the ICJ also pointed out that:

> The reference in paragraph 2 of [Article 24 of the UN Charter] to specific powers of the Security Council under certain chapters of the Charter does not exclude the existence of general powers to discharge the responsibilities conferred in paragraph I… the Members of the United Nations have conferred upon the Security Council powers commensurate with its responsibility for the maintenance of international peace and security.[22]

Even in the absence of a definition of international peace and security, the doctrine of implied powers of international organizations has been analysed in relation to SC actions. For instance, Henderson and Lubell argue that the SC power to adopt ceasefires is uncontroversial and that resolutions should be regarded as 'decisions' for the purposes of Article 25 of the UN Charter.[23]

Certain scholars maintain that the implied powers of an international organization's permanent organ are limited by the powers of other organs.[24] However, it has been pointed out that, in line with the Advisory Opinion of the Permanent Court of

---

[18]UN Charter, Art. 52, para. 1.

[19]UN Charter, Art. 53.

[20]Alvarez (2005), pp. 92–95.

[21]*Reparations for Injuries Suffered in the Service of the United Nations*, Advisory Opinion of 11 April 1949, [1949] ICJ Rep. 174, para. 182.

[22]*Legal Consequences for States of the Continued Presence of South Africa in Namibia (South West Africa) Notwithstanding Security Council Resolution 276*, Advisory Opinion of 21 June 1971, [1971] ICJ Rep. 16, para. 52.

[23]Henderson and Lubell (2013), pp. 379–380 (pointing out that 'a legally binding ceasefire could be implicitly adopted through the general implied powers of the UNSC in the realm of the maintenance of international peace and security,' at 380).

[24]Campbell (1983), p. 528.

International Justice (PCIJ) in *Greco-Turkish Agreement*,[25] 'the competence of each organ to determine the scope of its respective powers is self-referential and self-judging, measured only against the aims it pursues.'[26] Accordingly, it turns out that, as long as the political organs of the UN exercise different powers employing a variety of instruments on a case-by-case basis,[27] it is very difficult to identify the scope and limits of the implied powers of the SC. There is only a presumption about the limits of implied powers: namely, that actions are not *ultra vires* and, therefore, against the purposes of the UN.[28] Within this context, the legislative powers of the SC are also regarded as a form of implied powers.[29]

2.4 Legislative Powers

Scholars have pointed out that in recent years the SC has acquired legislative capacity.[30] In particular, resolution 1373(2001) is regarded as the point of departure from previous SC practice, which was characterized by resolutions adopted to address particular conflicts or situations. Specifically, resolution 1373 requires all states to take particular steps against international terrorism and to refrain from others. By the same token, resolution 1540(2004) obligates states to prevent non-state actors from developing, acquiring, manufacturing, possessing, transporting and transferring weapons of mass destruction.[31] Hence, scholars have pointed out that such resolutions, rather than being primarily of executive character, possess norms of general and abstract character and impose *erga omnes* obligations on states.[32] The empirical data shows that, notwithstanding the convincing interpretation given to the legal force of resolution 1373(2001) and resolution 1540 (2004), the legislative powers of the SC originated in the cold war period, where the SC exercised its legislative powers nearly 40 times.

The first instance of a SC resolution addressed to all states is resolution 145 (1960), which was adopted in relation to the situation in the Republic of the Congo. In the same period, on two other occasions it addressed a negative request—namely, that all states would refrain or desist from intervening in the domestic

[25] *Interpretation of Greco-Turkish Agreement of December 1st, 1926 (Final Protocol, Article IV)*, Advisory Opinion, 28 August 1928, PCIJ Publications (1928) Series B No. 16, at 20.

[26] Tsagourias (2011), p. 543.

[27] Tsagourias (2011).

[28] *Certain Expenses of the United Nations (Article 17, paragraph 2, of the Charter)*, Advisory Opinion, 20 July 1962, [1962] ICJ Rep. 151, at 168.

[29] Tsagourias (2011), p. 545.

[30] Powell (2007), pp. 166–170; Tsagourias 2011), p. 540. See also Szasz (2002), p. 901; Talmon (2005), p. 193.

[31] Tsagourias (2011), p. 540.

[32] Tsagourias (2011).

affairs of the Republic of the Congo[33]—while on one occasion it demanded a proactive role of all states in assisting the Organization of African Unity (OAU) in its efforts to help the Congo achieve national reconciliation in accordance with OAU resolutions.[34]

Overall, in the majority of cases the SC has resorted to the use of legislative powers in order to impose an economic[35] or military[36] embargo against a specific state. Thus, during the 1990s, it imposed a military and economic embargo against Iraq by demanding all states to freeze their commercial relationship with and military support to that country, with the exception of payments made for strictly humanitarian purposes and, in humanitarian circumstances, foodstuff.[37] Another case of military embargo is the one imposed against Yugoslavia in 1991, which was aimed at establishing peace and stability within the federal state.[38] A similar request was addressed to all states, UN members and non-members alike,[39] in order to impose a military embargo against South Africa.[40] In particular, the SC demanded states to adopt specific national legislation, including monitoring mechanisms, to implement its resolutions imposing the embargo.[41]

An example of economic embargo is the one imposed on Southern Rhodesia.[42] Like in the embargo against Iraq, the relevant SC resolutions contemplated humanitarian exceptions,[43] in addition to requiring all UN members not to accept a unilateral declaration of independence for Southern Rhodesia by the minority Government[44] or to recognize the illegal regime.[45] A similar request was addressed to all states to refrain to assist the Portuguese Government perpetrate its repression of the people of the Territories under its administration.[46]

In addition to the above, on three occasions the SC declared a domestic decision or document invalid. Specifically, in 1980 it affirmed that the Israeli 'basic law'

---

[33]Tsagourias (2011), para. 2, and Res. 199(1964), para. 1.

[34]Res. 199(1964), para. 5.

[35]Res. 661(1990), paras. 3–4; Res. 670(1990), paras. 3–4; and Res. 687(1991), paras. 24 and 29.

[36]Res. 687(1991), para. 24.

[37]Res. 661(1990), para. 4; and Res. 670(1990), para. 3.

[38]Res. 713(1991), para. 6; and Res. 724(1991), para. 5(a).

[39]Res. 558(1984), para. 3; and Res. 591(1986), para. 12.

[40]Res. 418(1977), para. 2; Res. 558(1984), para. 2; and Res. 591(1986), para. 4. See also Res. 418 (1977), para. 4; and Res. 591(1986), para. 5 (referring to nuclear weapons).

[41]Res. 591(1986), paras. 10–11.

[42]Res. 232(1966), para. 2; Res. 253(1968), paras. 3 (in furtherance of the objective of ending the rebellion) and 4–7; Res. 277(1970), para. 11 (referring to art 41 of the UN Charter); and Res. 333 (1973), para. 5 (containing a generic reference to States). Res. 253(1968), para. 4, also refers to member states of specialized agencies.

[43]Res. 253(1968), para. 4.

[44]Res. 202(1965), para. 3.

[45]Res. 277(1970), para. 2.

[46]Res. 218(1965), paras. 6 and 7 (the latter requesting states to inform the Secretary-General of any measure undertaken).

constituted a violation of international law and, as such, was null and void.[47] Likewise, in 1984 it declared the new racist Constitution of South Africa null and void as being contrary to the principles of the UN Charter.[48] In 1981, it also decided that the Israeli decision to impose its laws, jurisdiction and administration in the occupied Syrian Golan Heights was 'null and void and without international legal effect.'[49]

In the post-cold war period the SC resorted to its legislative powers twice as much as in the cold war period. Contrary to the cold war legislative resolutions, however, the post-cold war resolutions present a common structure that seems to have crystallized over the years. Specifically, SC requests are mainly addressed to all states and impose a commercial[50] or military[51] embargo on specific states with a view to fostering peace and security in a given state or region.[52] Often resolutions contain the starting date of the embargo[53] as well as a duty to report either to the Secretary-General[54] or to an *ad hoc* SC Committee.[55] However, humanitarian exceptions are not always contemplated.[56]

On other occasions, the SC has resorted to its legislative powers either to impose diplomatic restrictions with a certain state[57] or to oblige all states to cooperate with each other or with international tribunals for the purpose of reaching the goal of a specific SC resolution.[58] On one occasion, it has demanded all states to respect the measures established by an international organization.[59]

---

[47]Res. 478(1980), para. 2.

[48]Res. 554(1984), para. 2.

[49]Res. 497(1981), para. 1.

[50]Res. 1267(1999), para. 4, and Res. 1333(2000), paras. 5, 8 and 10–11 (Afghanistan); Res. 864 (1993), para. 19 (Angola); Res. 757(1992), paras. 4 and 7, Res. 820(1993), paras. 21–22 and 24–25, Res. 942(1994), paras. 7–12 and 16–18 (Bosnia and Herzegovina); Res. 841(1993), para. 5 (Haiti); Res. 1160(1998), para. 8 (Federal Republic of Yugoslavia); Res. 883(1993), para. 8 (Libya); and Res. 1306(2000), para. A1 (Sierra Leone).

[51]Res. 788(1992), para. 8 (Liberia); Res. 748(1992), para. 5, and Res. 883(1996), para. 5 (Libya); Res. 1011(1995), para. 9 (Rwanda); Res. 1132(1997), para. 6, and Res. 1171(1998), para. 2 (Sierra Leone); Res. 1298(2000), para. 6 (situation between Eritrea and Ethiopia); Res. 733(1992), para. 5 (Somalia); Res. 918(1994), para. 13 (UN Assistance Mission for Rwanda).

[52]Res. 1160(1998), para. 8; Res. 788(1992), para. 8; Res. 733(1992), para. 5.

[53]Res. 1267(1999), para. 3; Res. 748(1992), para. 3.

[54]Res. 864(1993), para. 24; Res. 757(1992), para. 12; Res. 841(1993), para. 13; Res. 748(1992), para 8; Res. 883(1993), para. 13; Res. 778(1992), para. 4; Res. 827(1993), para. 4; Res. 955 (1994), para. 2; Res. 1298(2000), para. 11; and Res. 917(1994), para. 13.

[55]Res. 1267(1999), para. 10; Res. 1333(2000), para. 20; Res. 748(1992), para. 4; Res. 883(1993), para. 6; Res. 1011(1995), para. 11; Res. 1171(1998), para. 4; and Res. 1306(2000), para. A8.

[56]Resolutions applying the humanitarian exception include: Res. 1267(1999), para. 4; Res. 757 (1992), para. 7; Res. 942(1994), para. 7(b).

[57]Res. 757(1992), para. 8; Res. 745(1992), para. 6; and Res. 1054(1996), para. 3.

[58]Res. 1019(1995), para. 8; Res. 827(1993), para. 4; Res. 955(1994), para. 2; and Res. 1192(1998), para. 4.

[59]Res. 788(1992) para 2.

The resolutions of the twenty-first century are significantly less in number, compared to the post-cold war ones, remaining within sixty. Nevertheless, in a continuum with the post-cold war resolutions, they establish an economic embargo, including on military products, against selected states,[60] and often include a duty of notification to an *ad hoc* Committee[61] as well as the duration of the embargo.[62] A distinctive trait of twenty-first century resolutions is that on one hand, they equally refer to 'all States'[63] or 'Member States'.[64] On the other hand, they contain a request addressed to all states to impose certain measures on targeted individuals and groups associated with them.[65] On one occasion, in a thematic resolution addressed to all states the SC has demanded to take action against a single state (Iran).[66]

The analysis above shows that most of the times the SC has exercised legislative powers, it has addressed its requests to 'all States'. Arguably, the expression is to be interpreted as referring to the Members of the UN, so long as there is explicit reference to non-member and other international actors when the resolution is not confined to the sphere of operation of the UN. For instance, an identical passage from resolution 757(1992) on Bosnia and Herzegovina, resolution 918 on the UN Assistance Mission for Rwanda and resolution 748(1996) on Libya reads:

> [The SC] Calls upon all States, *including States not members of the United Nations, and all international organizations*, to act strictly in accordance with the provisions of the present resolution.[67]

For the sake of consistency, the same perspective should be adopted in relation to those resolutions referring generically to 'States'.[68]

---

[60] Res. 1390(2002), para. 2 (Afghanistan); Res. 2134(2014), para. 32 (Central African Republic); Res. 1807(2008), para. 1 (Democratic Republic of the Congo); Res. 2153(2014), para. 1 (Ivory Coast); Res. 1343(2001), para. 5(a,b) and Res. 1521(2003), para. 2(a, b) (Liberia); Res. 1483 (2003), para. 23 (situation between Iraq and Kuwait); Res. 1591(2005), para. 3(e) (Sudan); Res. 2160(2014), para. 9 (threats to international peace and security caused by terrorist acts).

[61] Res. 1807(2008), para. 5; Res. 1737(2006), para. 19; Res. 1803(2008), para. 13; Res. 2182 (2014), para. 20.

[62] Res. 1478(2003), para. 17(a); Res. 1521(2003), paras. 6 and 10.

[63] Res. 1343(2001), para. 7(a); Res. 1478(2003), para. 28; Res. 1521(2003), para. 4(a); Res. 1493 (2003), para. 18. See also Res. 2166(2014), para. 11 (establishing a duty of cooperation among them) and Res. 1807(2008), para. 6 (addressed to 'all governments in the region').

[64] Res. 2134(2014), paras. 30 and 32; Res. 2174(2014), para. 10(b-d); Res. 2140(2014), paras. 11 and 15 ('all Member States); Res. 2182(2014), paras. 19–20 ('Member States'); Res. 2160 (2014), para. 24 ('relevant Member States').

[65] Res. 1636(2005), para. 3(a); Res. 1373(2001), paras. 1–2; Res. 1617(2005), para. 1; Res. 1735 (2006), para. 1; Res. 1904(2009), para. 1; Res. 2160(2014), para. 1.

[66] Res. 1737(2006), paras. 3–4, 6 and 12.

[67] Res. 757(1992), para. 11; Res. 918(1994), para. 15; and Res. 748(1996), para. 7 (emphasis added). See also Res. 1298(2000), para. 12 (referring to 'all States, relevant United Nations bodies and, as appropriate, other organizations and interested parties).

[68] Res. 333(1973), para. 5 on Southern Rhodesia; Res. 1011(1995), para. 11 on Rwanda; Res. 1298 (2000), para. 11 on the situation between Eritrea and Ethiopia.

The resolutions on combating international terrorism do not entirely fit in the scheme outlined above. Firstly, because of the wording used in the text of resolutions, it is difficult to establish whether the SC is exercising legislative powers. For example, a passage from resolution 1456(2003) reads:

> The Security Council calls upon States to… become a party, as a matter of urgency, to all relevant international conventions and protocols relating to terrorism.[69]

A nearly identical request is contained in a series of previous resolutions, where the SC explicitly referred to 'all States'.[70] Hence, it may be inferred that the passage above refers to member states, in line with the previous SC practice. This interpretation, however, is highly arguable. Other resolutions on the same subject matter are equally difficult to interpret. For example, resolution 2178(2014) at times refers to member states, requiring that their actions comply with international human rights, humanitarian and refugee law,[71] and at times to all states, demanding that all states ensure that their domestic laws and regulations prosecute and penalize certain criminal offenses.[72]

Secondly, the writing style is different from established practice, which would present the SC request to states as 'the Security Council decides that all States' or 'the Security Council requests that all States' comply with the terms of a specific SC resolution or set of resolutions.[73] Such a stylistic departure from SC practice is also coupled with the request that states comply with relevant international law rather than specific SC resolutions. A passage from resolution 1456(2003) reads:

> States must ensure that any measure taken to combat terrorism comply with all their obligations under international law, and should adopt such measures in accordance with international law, in particular international human rights, refugee, and humanitarian law.[74]

2.5 Conclusion

This chapter has provided an overview of the powers of the SC. Particular emphasis has been placed on the conceptualization and development of legislative powers over the seven decades of SC practice. The systematic analysis of SC behavioural patterns shows that the use of legislative powers traces back to the cold-war period and reaches a peak in the 1990s, although the most poignant use of such powers has

[69] Res. 1456(2003), Annex, para. 2(a).

[70] Res. 1373(2001), para. 3(d), and Res. 1377(2001), Annex, para. 10.

[71] Res. 2178(2014), para. 5.

[72] Res. 2178(2014), para. 6.

[73] The strongest request in this sense is to be found in the thematic resolutions on the protection of civilians in armed conflict where the SC demanded that 'all States and parties to armed conflict fully implement all relevant decisions of the Security Council.' See Res. 1674(2006), para. 10, and Res. 1894(2009), para. 6.

[74] Res. 1456(2003), Annex, para. 6.

been made in the twenty-first century, especially in the area of international terrorism. Bearing in mind the topics discussed in this chapter, Chap. 3 provides an original reconstruction of the use of international law by the SC from 1946 to 2014.

Bibliography

Abass, Ademola. 2004. *Regional organizations and the development of collective security*. Oxford: Hart Publishing.

Alvarez, José. 2005. *International organizations as law-makers*. New York: Oxford University Press.

Campbell, A.I.L. 1983. The limits on the powers of international organizations. *International and Comparative Law Quarterly* 32: 523–533.

Chesterman, Simon, Thomas M. Franck, and David M. Malone. 2008. *Law and practice of the United Nations—documents and commentary*. New York: Oxford University Press.

de Wet, Erika. 2004. *The Chapter VII powers of the United Nations Security Council*. Oxford: Hart Publishing.

Henderson, Christian, and Noam Lubell. 2013. The contemporary legal nature of UN Security Council ceasefire resolutions. *Leiden Journal of International Law* 26: 369–397.

Malone, David M. 2008. Security council. In *The Oxford handbook on the United Nations*, ed. Thomas G. Weiss, and Sam Daws, 117–135. New York: Oxford University Press.

Powell, Cathleen. 2007. The legal authority of the United Nations Security Council. In *Security and human rights*, eds. Benjamin J. Goold and Liora Lazarus, 157–183. Oxford: Hart Publishing.

Szasz, Paul C. 2002. The Security Council starts legislating. *American Journal of International Law* 96: 901–905.

Talmon, Stefan. 2005. The Security Council as world legislature. *American Journal of International Law* 99: 175–193.

Tsagourias, Nicholas. 2011. Security Council legislation, Article 2(7) of the UN Charter, and the principle of subsidiarity. *Leiden Journal of International Law* 24: 539–559.

Chapter 3
Analysis of Security Council's Practice

3.1 Introduction

This chapter introduces the empirical framework for assessing Security Council (SC) practice. Section 3.2 outlines the research design, including the methodology used for data collection and the reasons for selecting specific categories of SC resolutions. The remaining sections examine the extent to which the SC relies upon international law. By determining which rules of international law have been utilised by the SC in its resolutions and how they interact with each other, these sections aim to conceptualise the legal basis that justifies SC actions beyond the UN Charter provisions establishing its mandate.

3.2 An Empirical Framework of Analysis

Empirical scholarship on SC practice is still in its infancy. Existent contributions have built a taxonomy of SC decisions with a view to finding significant selection effects.[1] Other scholars have then used the results of the empirical analysis as a platform to assess the degree of compliance of SC decisions with international human rights standards.[2] This chapter provides a deeper understanding of the rationale behind the adoption of SC resolutions. By mapping the rules and principles of international law referred to in the text of SC resolutions, the proposed analysis attempts to conceptualize the legal mind of the SC.

The basis of the present research is quantitative and consists in coding and analyzing 2,195 resolutions adopted by the SC from 1946 to 2014. The full text of

[1]Deplano (2014), p. 139.
[2]Vargiu and Deplano (2014), pp. 520–541.

R. Deplano, *The Strategic Use of International Law by the United Nations Security Council*, SpringerBriefs in Law, DOI 10.1007/978-3-319-21281-4_3

resolutions is reported in the SC Annual Report to the General Assembly, which gathers all the questions considered by the SC during the year, as well as in the digital archive developed in 1995 by the UN Department of Public Information, which is freely available and provides direct access, via hypertext links, to each SC resolution since 1946.[3]

The research methodology adopted is based on the textual analysis of all SC resolutions, from the origins up to 31 December 2014. In order to establish the extent to which international law influences the politics of the SC and vice versa, a custom-built database has been created. The coding method is organized in two parts. Firstly, in order to identify and classify existent categories of SC resolutions, individual resolutions have been grouped into different categories by using the descriptive formulation provided for all resolutions in the digital archive of the SC. Secondly, the provisions of international law expressly mentioned in the text of resolutions have been identified and analyzed, in turn, in context of three historical periods of time—namely, the origins and cold war period (1946–1991), the post-cold war period (1992–2000), and the twenty-first century (2001–2014)—which are regarded as having had a distinctive impact on the functioning of the SC.[4]

The following sections examine the extent to which the SC relies upon international law. They show evidence of the type of international legal instruments referred to in the text of resolutions. Such instruments have been divided into two groups. They include UN documents such as SC resolutions, SC Presidential statements (PRSTs), General Assembly resolutions, and reports of the Secretary-General on one hand, and primary sources, such as treaties concluded between states and customary international law (CIL) on the other hand. The analysis also considers generic reference to international law, including international humanitarian law, international human rights law, refugee law and international standards.

Sometimes the same source is cited more than once in the same paragraph of a resolution. For the purpose of this study, only the first citation is taken into account. Furthermore, since the inquiry is restricted to evaluating the use of international legal instruments by the SC, generic reference to human rights or the rule of law is not reported.

3.3 Origins and Cold War Period

In the period between 1946 and 1991 the SC adopted 725 resolutions. Overall, the distinctive trait of the cold war resolutions is the importance attached to the purposes and principles of the UN Charter. There is also a complete absence of

[3]<www.un.org/en/sc/documents/> accessed 18 June 2015.

[4]Bourandonis (2005).

cross-references to PRSTs on either the same subject matter of individual resolutions or related ones.

Several resolutions do not contain any reference to international legal documents[5] while a significant number of sets of re-cited resolutions refer only to various instruments of UN law, mostly previous SC resolutions and GA resolutions. Among them, the thirteen resolutions on the situation between Angola and South Africa stand out as being entirely based on reliance upon the purposes and principles of the UN Charter and relevant resolutions of the United Nations.[6] A great number of resolutions also refer to international treaties.[7] In particular, the resolutions on hostage taking contain the highest number of references to international treaties. Conversely, reference to customary international law is confined to resolution 620 (1988) on the situation between Iraq and Iran.[8]

Fourteen sets of resolutions contain a generic reference to international law. They establish that a certain situation violating international law or international legal standards constitutes an actual or potential breach of international peace and security while on other occasions they require the parties involved in a dispute to take actions according to international law.[9] Within this context, on one hand, the re-cited resolutions on the situation between Iraq and Kuwait contain the highest number of references to international law. On the other hand, the resolutions on the situation between Iraq and Israel and those on Israel and Tunisia contain expressions such as 'norms of (international) conduct' and 'internationally accepted objectives' whose interpretation is ambivalent.[10]

The re-cited resolutions on hostage taking, the situation between Iraq and Iran, and especially those on Iraq and Kuwait mention international humanitarian law. Conversely, international human rights law is never mentioned, although a

[5]Relevant sets of re-cited resolutions include: appointment of the Secretary-General, question relating to the Dominican Republic, Laos, Taiwan (Formosa), hijacking of commercial aircrafts and the Corfu Channel incidents.

[6]Two resolutions also contain a generic reference to international conventions on the status of refugees and international law. See Res. 571(1985), para. 5; Res. 545(1983), Preamble para. 2, and para. 1 of the operative part.

[7]See, for instance, the resolutions on the situation between Afghanistan and Pakistan, Angola and those on the International Court of Justice.

[8]Res. 620(1988), para. 2. The set of resolutions on Iraq and Iran stands out for the variety of international legal sources referred to by the SC, which include various UN documents, international treaties, generic reference to international law and, as mentioned above in the text, CIL.

[9]Most of the times resolutions refer to 'international law.' However, other resolutions contain expressions such as 'international rights and obligations', 'international obligations', 'principles of international law' and 'internationally accepted norms'. See, for instance, Res. 395(1976), para. 6; Res. 568(1985), para. 6; Res. 527(1982), para. 2; Res. 580(1985), para. 4; Res. 640(1989), para. 6; and Res. 581(1986), para. 9.

[10]Res. 487(1981), paras. 1 and 4; Res. 573(1985), para. 1; and Res. 611(1988), para. 1.

restricted number of sets of resolutions contain multiple references to the Universal Declaration of Human Rights, which, in this specific period of time, can be regarded as the reference document in the field of human rights.[11]

Finally, two resolutions seem to have unique features. On one hand, resolution 497(1981) refers to the UN Charter provisions, principles of international law and SC resolutions as if they were on an equal footing,[12] thus granting the resolutions of the SC the same legal status of formal sources of international law, as established in Article 38 of the ICJ Statute. On the other hand, resolution 668(1990) turns out to be the most politicized one. Paragraph 1 of the resolution reads:

> [The SC] Endorses the framework for a comprehensive political settlement of the Cambodia conflict and encourages *the continuing efforts of China, France, the Union of Soviet Socialist Republics, the United Kingdom of Great Britain and Northern Ireland and the United States of America in this regard.*[13]

Similar statements stressing the role of the permanent members of the SC as the sole judges of disputes concerning threats to international peace and security can be found in the resolution on non-nuclear weapon states[14] and those on Palestine.[15] This interpretation seems to be confirmed by a strand of resolutions pointing out that the lack of unanimity among the permanent five members has prevented the SC from exercising its primary responsibility for the maintenance of international peace and security.[16]

3.4 Post-cold War Period

In the period between 1992 and 2000 the SC has adopted 608 resolutions. On one hand, they differ from the cold war period resolutions in two ways. Firstly, only the set of resolutions on the appointment of the Secretary-General do not contain any reference to international legal materials. Secondly, the attention given to the purposes and principles of the UN Charter during the origins and cold war period is now replaced by constant reference to international law, including international humanitarian, human rights and refugee law. On the other hand, like the cold war

[11]See resolutions on Namibia, South Africa, territories occupied by Israel and West Africa.

[12]Res. 497(1981), Preamble, para. 2.

[13]Emphasis added.

[14]Res. 255(1968), para. 1.

[15]Res. 42(1948), para. 2 ('[The SC] Resolves to call on *the permanent members of the Council* to consult and to inform the Security Council regarding the situation with respect to Palestine and to make, *as the result of such consultations*, recommendations to it regarding the guidance and instructions which the Council might usefully give to the Palestine Commission with a view to implementing the resolution of the General Assembly.' Emphasis added).

[16]See resolutions on Cuba (complaint by), the Democratic Republic of the Congo, Egypt (compliant by), Hungary, the situation between India and Pakistan, international peace and security and compliant by Lebanon and Jordan.

resolutions, a great number of re-cited resolutions mention only various types of UN documents, such as relevant SC resolutions and reports of the Secretary-General.

The number of re-cited resolutions either calling for compliance with international law or denouncing a violation of relevant rules and principles of international law are twice as much as those in the cold war period.[17] In addition, forty groups of resolutions contain multiple references of the rules of international humanitarian law, mostly to denounce a violation thereof, with the total of citations amounting to over two hundred.[18] In a similar vein, resolutions also contain a generic reference to international human rights law[19] and refugee law,[20] although their combined number of citations is one quarter of the resolutions on humanitarian law, and it is spread across only twenty groups of resolutions. Finally, other resolutions address human rights and humanitarian issues either in the form of thematic resolutions—especially those on children, women and civilians[21]—or resolutions containing a cross-reference to the thematic resolutions.[22]

Customary international law is also recognized as a source of international obligations. A passage from resolution 1067(1996) reads:

> [The SC] Condemns the use of weapons against civil aircraft in flight as being incompatible with elementary considerations of humanity, *the rules of customary international law as codified in article 3*bis *of the Chicago Convention*, and the standards and recommended practices set out in the annexes of the Convention.[23]

The same resolution also refers to 'the principle, *recognized under customary international law*, concerning the non-use of weapons against [civil] aircraft in flight'[24] while resolution 937(1994) on the UN Observation mission in Georgia

---

[17]Provisions containing a generic reference to international law utilise expressions such as 'international law', 'rules and principles of international law' and 'standards of international law'. See, Res. 1170(1998), Preamble, para. 10; Res. 1261(1999), paras. 2–3, 13, 15 and 18; and Res. 978(1995), paras. 1 and 5, respectively.

[18]See, for example, the resolutions on Africa, Angola, Bosnia and Herzegovina, the Democratic Republic of the Congo, Kosovo, Liberia, the Middle East, Rwanda, Sierra Leone and Somalia.

[19]See, for instance, Res. 1213(1998), para. 7 (Angola); Res. 1319(2000), para. 3 (East Timor); Res. 1034(1995), para. 6 (Former Yugoslavia); and Res. 1270 (1999), paras. 15 and 22.

[20]They include the group of resolutions on Angola, children and armed conflict, East Timor, Sierra Leone and the situation between Eritrea and Ethiopia.

[21]Res. 1261(1999) and Res. 1314(2000) (children); Res. 1325(2000) (women); and Res. 1265 (1999) and Res. 1296(2000).

[22]See, for example, Res. 1314(2000), Preamble, para. 2; Res. 1304(2000), Preamble, para. 1; Res. 1332(2000), Preamble, para. 1; Res. 1327(2000), Annex, para. V-6; Res. 1270(1999), Preamble, para. 2; and Res. 1325(2000), Preamble, para. 1, and para. 12 (operative part) mentioning the thematic resolutions on civilians; Res. 1327(2000), Annex, para. V-8 mentioning the resolution on women; and Res. 1265(1999), para. 19, and Res. 1325(2000), Preamble, para. 1 mentioning the resolutions on children.

[23]Res. 1067(1996), para. 6.

[24]Res. 1067(1996), Preamble, para. 5.

refers to 'established principles and practices of the United Nations,' which may be regarded as evocative of *usus* and *opinio juris*.[25]

Other resolutions seem to have a direct impact on the idea of legal force of SC resolutions and the development of international law through the SC resolutions. Examples of the first category include resolution 1265(1999) on the protection of civilians in armed conflict, which refers to relevant provisions of the UN Charter, relevant SC resolutions and relevant international instruments as equal sources of obligation.[26] In the same vein, resolution 833(1993) requires Iraq and Kuwait to act in accordance with international law and relevant SC resolutions.[27] Resolution 1269 (1999) on the responsibility of the SC in maintaining international peace and security belongs to the second category, as it takes an active role in the effort of crystallizing existent international law on terrorism and of promoting the adoption of fresh international legislation on the same topic. The relevant passages of the resolution read:

> [The SC] Support[s] the efforts to promote universal participation in and implementation of the existing international anti-terrorist conventions, *as well as to develop new international instruments to counter the terrorist threat*.[28][...]

> [The SC] Calls upon all States to implement fully the international anti-terrorist conventions to which they are parties, encourages all States to consider as a matter of priority adhering to those to which they are not parties, and encourages also the speedy adoption of the pending conventions.[29]

Three other individual resolutions have distinctive features. On one hand, resolution 1172(1998) on international peace and security contains the only, indirect reference to the role of the permanent members of the SC in influencing the politics of the SC.[30] On the other hand, resolutions 1165(1998) and 970(1995) contain a mistake in the text of the resolution.[31]

---

[25]Res. 937(1994), para. 4.

[26]Res. 1265(1999), para. 4.

[27]Res. 833(1993), para. 5.

[28]Res. 1269(1999), Preamble, para. 5.

[29]Res. 1269(1999), Preamble, para. 2.

[30]Res. 1172(1998), para. 2 ('[The SC] Endorses the Joint Communique *issued by the Foreign Ministers of China, France, the Russian Federation, the United Kingdom of Great Britain and Northern Ireland and the United States of America* at their meeting in Geneva on 4 June 1998 (S/1998/473)').

[31]In the UN website, resolution 1165(1998) is described as being about the International Criminal Tribunal for the Former Yugoslavia whereas it deals with a decision about the International Criminal Tribunal for Rwanda. See <http://www.un.org/en/sc/documents/resolutions/1998.shtml> accessed 18 June 2015. Likewise, resolution 970(1995) on Yugoslavia and Bosnia and Herzegovina contains an incorrect citation of a resolution (at para. 4).

3.5 The Twenty-First Century

In the period between 2001 and 2014 the SC has adopted 761 resolutions. The overall results show that the majority of citations concern UN documents in general and SC resolutions in particular. The latter are equally divided between resolutions on the same subject-matter of the resolution under scrutiny, and resolutions addressing related topics. Re-cited SC resolutions are often accompanied by reference to related PRSTs. In general, the Preamble contains a higher number of citations than the operative part of resolutions.

The most cited sets of resolutions address thematic issues—namely, women and peace and security, children in armed conflict, protection of civilians in armed conflicts and threats to international peace and security caused by terrorist acts. They appear to have gained a special status among the sample of SC resolutions examined and, therefore, will be discussed separately.[32] Conversely, the resolutions on the admission of new members to the United Nations, those providing recommendations for the appointment of the new Secretary-General, the one containing a tribute to the outgoing Secretary-General[33] and those establishing a date of election to fill a vacancy in the International Court of Justice (ICJ) do not contain any reference to international legal documents.

On a number of occasions, compliance with relevant SC resolutions is required in absolute terms.[34] Whether this consolidated practice constitutes a precedent, at least with regard to resolutions referring to previous SC resolutions on the same subject matter,[35] is contested, although the answer seems to be negative.[36] Likewise, re-cited SC resolutions do not appear to contribute to the creation or development of CIL,[37] though it is worthy to note that at times they refer to established practice of the United Nations.[38] As reported in the most recent resolution on Libya:

---

[32]See Chap. 5.

[33]Res. 1733(2006).

[34]Res. 1887(2009), para. 10; Res. 1894(2009), paras. 1 and 6; Res. 1904(2009), para. 44; Res. 1963(2010), para. 17; Res. 2009(2011), para. 11; Res. 2035(2012), Preamble, para. 15; Res. 2068 (2012), para. 1; Res. 2075(2012), para. 2; Res. 2104(2013), para. 5; 2126(2013), para. 6.

[35]Res. 1882(2009), Preamble, para. 10, and para. 7; Res. 1929(2010), paras. 6 and 16; Res. 1998 (2011), para. 9; Res. 2068(2012), para. 3; Res. 2075(2012), para. 2.

[36]Res. 2118(2013), Preamble, para. 14. *Contra* see Res. 1904(2009), para. 1 (establishing duties of compliance with previous SC resolutions on international terrorism for both UN members and non-member states).

[37]Res. 1918(2010), Preamble, para. 4 ('underscoring that resolution 1897 shall not be considered as establishing customary international law'). See also Res. 1897(2009), para. 8; Res. 1950(2010), para. 8; Res. 2020(2011), para. 10; Res. 2077(2012), para. 13; and Res. 2125(2013), para. 13 ('underscoring that this resolution shall not be considered as establishing customary international law'); Res. 1976(2011), Preamble, para. 9; Res. 2015(2011), Preamble, para. 7.

[38]Res. 1457(2003), paras. 12 and 16 (Democratic Republic of the Congo).

> [T]he authorization provided by paragraph 5 of this resolution applies only with respect to vessels that are the subject of a designation made by the Committee pursuant to paragraph 11 and shall not affect the rights or obligations or responsibilities of Member States under international law, including rights or obligations under the United Nations Convention on the Law of the Sea, including the general principle of exclusive jurisdiction of a flag state over its vessels on the high seas, with respect to other vessels and in any other situation, and underscores in particular that *this resolution shall not be considered as establishing customary international law*.[39]

However, with regard to the legal force of resolutions, they appear to stay on an equal footing with primary sources of international law. A passage from resolution 2087(2013), for example, reads:

> Recognizing the freedom of all States to explore and use outer space in accordance with international law, including restrictions imposed by relevant Security Council resolutions.[40]

In more absolute terms, resolution 1441(2002) on the situation between Iraq and Kuwait establishes that 'the resolutions of the Security Council constitute the governing standard of Iraqi compliance.'[41]

Nonetheless, certain treaty provisions are recognized as the standard of international legality in certain fields and might be successful in mitigating, to a certain extent, the discretionary powers of the SC. Prominent examples are the Treaty of Non-Proliferation of Nuclear Weapons (NPT),[42] the UN Convention on the Law of the Sea (UNCLOS),[43] the Geneva Conventions,[44] and the purposes and principles of the UN Charter.[45]

The analysis also shows that particular sets of resolutions stand out either for the abundance or the paucity of the sources of international law other than UN

---

[39]Res. 2146(2014), para. 9 (emphasis added).

[40]Res. 2087(2013), Preamble, para. 2.

[41]Res. 1441(2002), Preamble, para. 11.

[42]Res. 1887(2009), paras. 6 ('Underlining that the NPT remains the cornerstone of the nuclear non-proliferation regime and the essential foundation for the pursuit of nuclear disarmament and for the peaceful uses of nuclear energy') and 7 ('Reaffirming its firm commitment to the NPT and its conviction that the international nuclear non-proliferation regime should be maintained and strengthened to ensure its effective implementation').

[43]Res. 2018(2011), Preamble, para. 6 ('Affirming that international law, as reflected in the United Nations Convention on the Law of the Sea of 10 December 1982, in particular its articles 100, 101 and 105, sets out the legal framework applicable to countering piracy and armed robbery at sea, as well as other ocean activities'). See also Res. 2039(2012), Preamble, para. 5; Res. 1897(2009), Preamble, para. 4; Res. 1950(2010), Preamble, para. 6; Res. 2020(2011), Preamble, para. 7; Res. 2077(2012), Preamble, para. 7; Res. 2125(2013), Preamble, para. 9; Res. 1918(2010), Preamble, para. 3; Res. 1976(2011), Preamble, para. 8; and Res. 2015(2011), Preamble, para. 6.

[44]Res. 1894(2009), Preamble, para. 4 ('the Geneva Conventions of 1949, which together with their Additional Protocols constitute the basis for the legal framework for the protection of civilians in armed conflict').

[45]Res. 2014(2011), para. 9; Res. 2051(2012), para. 15; and Res. 1894(2009), Preamble, para. 2.

documents referred to in the text of those resolutions. Resolutions on Somalia as well as those drawing on the reports of the Secretary-General on Sudan and South Sudan are examples of the first type. They both address situations classified as breaches of international peace and security and represent the cusp of a trend in which SC resolutions addressing situations taking place in Africa rely heavily upon international legal instruments as the preferred means for eliciting compliance of their addressees.[46] Most notably, the resolutions on the reports of the Secretary-General on Sudan and South Sudan contain a well-proportioned amount of reference to sources of international law in both the Preamble and the operative part of resolutions. Sources referred to include treaties, various UN documents and generic reference to international law, including international humanitarian and human rights law in equal measure. On the other hand, the distinctive trait of resolutions on Somalia is that they are the only ones, together with resolution 2146 (2014) on Libya, to mention CIL and, contrary to the majority of SC resolutions under scrutiny, place more emphasis on international human rights law rather than international humanitarian law.

Resolutions on Afghanistan and threats to international peace and security caused by terrorist acts pertain to the second type. Reference to international treaties is virtually absent in the latter, with the Bonn Agreement of 2005 on Afghanistan mentioned once in the Preamble to resolution 1988(2011)[47] and relevant conventions on international terrorism mentioned twice in the Preamble[48] and four times in the operative part of resolutions.[49] This set of resolutions is also characterized by a continuous reference, both in the Preamble and in the operative part, to previous SC resolutions on Afghanistan and general issues relating to sanctions. Resolution 1904(2009) also dictates that all States, UN members and non-members alike, must take the measures to combat international terrorism as imposed by previous SC resolutions.[50] Despite sporadic reference to international law, humanitarian law, international human rights law and refugee law in the Preamble, however, it is hard to single out the parameter of legality adopted by the SC to justify its actions other than SC resolutions themselves.

Resolutions on Afghanistan, on the other hand, tend to supply the paucity of reference to international treaties with great attention to SC resolutions on women,

---

[46]See resolutions on the Democratic Republic of the Congo, Ivory Coast, Mali, Peace and security in Africa, Sudan and Sudan/South Sudan. *Contra* see resolutions on Liberia and Sierra Leone.

[47]Res. 1988(2011), para. 6.

[48]Res. 1373(2001), Preamble, para. 7; and Res. 2133(2014), Preamble, para. 4. See also Res. 1450 (2002), Preamble, para. 2 (mentioning the International Convention for the suppression of Unlawful Acts against the Safety of Aviation).

[49]Res. 1373(2001), para. 3(e); Res. 1566(2004), paras. 3–4; and Res. 1368(2001), para. 4 (relevant anti-terrorism conventions).

[50]Res. 1904(2009), para. 1.

children, and civilians as well as resolutions on threats to international peace and security caused by terrorist acts. Most of the resolutions contain various references to international law, including international humanitarian law and international human rights law, in general. However, in spite of this, it appears that only the former set of resolutions—women, children, and civilians—may be regarded as the legal basis of SC actions,[51] in addition to the UN Charter provisions establishing the SC mandate.

Finally, the empirical results show that two individual resolutions possess unique features. The first one is resolution 1929(2010) on nuclear non-proliferation in Iran. It stands out as the most politicized of the resolutions under scrutiny as it establishes that to restore the confidence of the international community, the strategy for resolving the Iranian nuclear issue through peaceful means must conform to proposals made by the five permanent members of the SC.[52] The second one is resolution 2059(2012) on the situation in the Middle East. In this resolution, it is striking the absence of any reference to any previous SC resolutions, either on the same subject matter or related ones, as well as to international treaties.

3.6 Conclusion

The findings of the analysis show that the SC relies upon a wide range of sources of international law. References to international legal materials in the text of resolutions, either in the form of primary or secondary sources, abound and, accordingly, it may *prima facie* be assumed that they exercise some restrictive influence over the discretionary powers of the SC. However, apart from the field of international terrorism, where the SC resolutions serve the double function of crystallizing existent norms and facilitating the production of new ones, re-cited resolutions do not constitute a precedent, thus making the effort of establishing a parameter of legality of SC action an ambiguous task. What is remarkable, however, is the development of four strands of SC thematic resolutions which are solidly grounded on international law and have been used to justify SC action on several occasions.

[51]Resolution 2189(2014) does not refer to any previous SC resolution and, therefore, represents an exception.

[52]Res. 1929(2010), Preamble, para. 15, and para. 32 (operative part).

Bibliography

Bourandonis, Dimitris. 2005. *The history and politics of UN Security Council reform*. New York: Routledge.

Deplano, Rossana. 2014. Building a taxonomy of UN Security Council decisions: a biased compliance with the UN Charter obligations? *State Practice and International Law Journal* 1: 139–160.

Vargiu, Paolo, and Deplano, Rossana. 2014. The human rights dimension of UN Security Council resolutions. In *Essays on human rights: a celebration of the life of Dr. Janusz Kochanowski*, ed. Jo Carby-Hall, 520–541. Warsaw: Ius et Lex.

Chapter 4
The Age of International Law in Security Council's Practice

4.1 Introduction

This chapter provides a detailed account of the specific content and legal effects of the resolutions addressing thematic issues. In particular, this chapter addresses two questions: do the Security Council (SC) thematic resolutions complement existent rules and principles of international law? Do they create new obligations, thus contributing to the development of international law? The analysis shows that of all the thematic resolutions adopted by the SC since 1946, the group of resolutions on women, children, protection of civilians and international terrorism represent the hallmark of twenty-first century SC practice. Since their introduction, they have been constantly referred to by the SC in resolutions addressing other topics along with other sources of international and UN law. The analysis also shows that the normative content of the group of resolutions on women, children and civilians cannot be regarded as either a form of implied powers or *ultra vires*: they represent a form of 'self-imposed duties'. Conversely, the resolutions on international terrorism have a restricted geographical application and serve the function of both crystallizing existent norms and facilitating the adoption of new ones in the same field.

4.2 The Relevance of Thematic Resolutions in Security Council's Practice: A Conceptual Map

The scope of the SC mandate has expanded over time in order to cope with the challenges posed by new forms of internal and transnational threats to international peace and security.[1] The most evident proof of this evolution is the introduction on the SC agenda of thematic resolutions. In particular, two groups of resolutions have

[1]Reisman (1993).

R. Deplano, *The Strategic Use of International Law by the United Nations Security Council*, SpringerBriefs in Law, DOI 10.1007/978-3-319-21281-4_4

become dominant in the daily work of the SC and appear to constitute the basis, at least partially, of the legitimacy of SC actions. They include the resolutions on women, children and civilians on one hand, and international terrorism on the other hand. The growing importance of thematic resolutions in general, and of resolutions on women in particular, is stressed in a passage from resolution 2122(2013):

> [The SC] Expresses its intention to increase its attention to women, peace and security in all relevant thematic areas of work on its agenda, including in particular Protection of civilians in armed conflict, Post-conflict peacebuilding, The promotion and strengthening of the rule of law in the maintenance of international peace and security, Peace and security in Africa, Threats to international peace and security caused by terrorist acts, and Maintenance of international peace and security.[2]

The following sub-sections address, in turn, the thematic resolutions on civilians, women, children and international terrorism. However, it must be noted here that the SC has adopted certain thematic resolutions since its early days of activity, though not in a systematic way.

The empirical data show that during the origins and cold-war period, for example, the SC adopted resolutions on armaments, atomic energy, hostage taking, international peace and security, marking of explosives, non-nuclear weapons states and even a resolution on the relations between Great Powers.[3]

The thematic resolutions adopted by the SC during the post-cold war period include those on the effective role of the SC in maintaining international peace and security, HIV/AIDS and peacekeeping operations, international peace and security, the responsibility of the SC in maintaining international peace and security, and the use of nuclear weapons.[4] The first resolutions on women, children, civilians and international terrorism were also adopted in this period.[5]

Finally, thematic resolutions adopted during the twenty-first century include those on the cooperation between the UN and regional and sub-regional organizations in maintaining international peace and security, general issues relating to

---

[2]Res. 2122(2013), para. 3. See also PRST 2014/21, para. 5 (establishing that 'The Council reiterates its intention to increase its attention to women, peace and security as a cross-cutting subject in all relevant thematic areas of work on its agenda, including on threats to international peace and security caused by terrorist acts'). In relation to children, the SC stated that 'the protection of children in armed conflict should be an important aspect of any comprehensive strategy to resolve conflict and build peace;' Res. 2143(2014), Preamble, para. 8.

[3]Res. 97(1952) and previous ones (armaments); Res. 74(1949) (atomic energy); Res. 638(1989) and previous ones (hostage taking); 500(1982) and previous ones (international peace and security); Res. 635(1989) (marking of explosives); Res. 255(1968) (non-nuclear weapons states); and Res. 135(1960).

[4]Res. 1318(2000) (effective role of the SC in maintaining international peace and security); Res. 1308(2000) (HIV/AIDS and peacekeeping operations); Res. 1172(1998) (international peace and security); Res. 1269(1999) (responsibility of the SC in maintaining international peace and security); and Res. 984(1995) (use of nuclear weapons).

[5]See Sect. 4.3.

sanctions, maintenance of international peace and security, non-proliferation of weapons of mass destruction, post-conflict peacebuilding and the role of the SC in the prevention of armed conflict,[6] in addition to the resolutions on women, children, civilians and international terrorism.[7]

The full implementation of the latter group of resolutions by all parties to armed conflicts has become one main focus of SC activity. As Table 4.1 shows, thirty-three groups of non-thematic resolutions mention, at least once, the resolutions on women, twenty-seven groups of resolutions refer to the resolutions on children and twenty-three groups of re-cited resolutions cite those on civilians while only fifteen groups of resolutions refer to those on international terrorism. A shared characteristic of all the non-thematic resolutions above-mentioned is that the thematic resolutions are mainly referred to in the Preamble rather than in the operative part of the text of resolutions. Another commonality is that the entirety of citations of thematic resolutions is contained in other, minor thematic resolutions or in resolutions addressing issues taking place in Africa and the Middle East, with the exception of the resolutions on Haiti and Timor-Leste. This suggests that the normative value assigned to the four major groups of thematic resolutions is closer to the one of *lex ferenda* rather than *lex lata*. Moreover, the geographical distribution of resolutions referring to the thematic ones raises suspicion of selection bias in the practice of the SC.[8]

4.3 Conceptualizing Thematic Resolutions

This section examines the main features of four sets of SC resolutions addressing thematic issues. As shown in Sect. 4.2 above, they are regularly referred to in the text of most SC resolutions as well as PRSTs, and appear to set a standard of legality of SC actions. The analysis aims at establishing whether the SC resolutions on civilians, children, women and international terrorism are able to limit the discretionary powers of the SC. To that end, each set of resolutions is taken into consideration individually and examined in its entirety since its introduction on the SC agenda.

[6]Res. 2033(2012) and previous one (cooperation between the UN and regional and sub-regional organizations in maintaining international peace and security); Res. 1732(2006) and previous one (general issues relating to sanctions); Res. 2154(2014) (maintenance of international peace and security); Res. 2055(2012) and previous one (non-proliferation of weapons of mass destruction); Res. 1947(2010) and previous ones (post-conflict peacebuilding); and Res. 1366(2001) (role of the SC in the prevention of armed conflict).

[7]See Sect. 4.3.

[8]As discussed in Chap. 5.

Table 4.1 Number of citations of thematic resolutions on women, children, civilians and international terrorism

Non-thematic resolutions	Women		Children		Civilians		International terrorism	
	Pream.	Op.part	Pream.	Op.part	Pream.	Op.part	Pream.	Op.part
Afghanistan	18	11	15	7	22	0	31	23
Burundi	8	2	7	1	7	1	0	0
Chad, Central African Republic and the sub-region	4	0	3	0	4	0	0	0
Children in armed conflict	3	0	–	–	3	0	0	0
Cooperation between the UN and regional and sub-regional organizations	1	0	1	0	0	0	0	0
Democratic republic of the Congo	17	7	18	4	17	0	0	0
General issues relating to sanctions	0	0	0	0	0	0	1	0
Great Lakes region	1	0	1	0	0	0	0	0
Guinea-Bissau	3	5	0	0	0	0	0	0
Haiti	3	13	1	10	1	4	0	0
High-level meeting of the SC: combating international terrorism	0	0	0	0	0	0	3	0
Implementation of the report of the Panel on UN Peace Operations (S/2000/809)	1	0	0	0	1	0	0	0
Iraq	3	0	2	0	0	0	6	0
Ivory Coast	23	11	21	6	19	0	0	0
Letters from the Secretary-General	7	0	6	0	0	0	0	0
Liberia	6	1	1	1	0	0	0	0
Libya	5	0	5	0	5	0	0	0
Maintenance of international peace and security	1	0	1	0	0	0	0	0
Maintenance of international peace and security: conflict prevention	1	0	0	0	0	0	1	0
Maintenance of international peace and security: security sector reform	1	0	1	0	1	0	0	0
Mali	0	4	0	4	0	4	3	5
Middle East	9	0	1	1	2	0	10	5

(continued)

Table 4.1 (continued)

Non-thematic resolutions	Women		Children		Civilians		International terrorism	
	Pream.	Op.part	Pream.	Op.part	Pream.	Op.part	Pream.	Op.part
Non-proliferation of weapons of mass destruction	0	0	0	0	0	0	1	2
Peace and security in Africa	1	1	2	1	0	1	1	3
Protection of civilians in armed conflict	3	0	2	1	–	–	0	0
Protection of UN and associated personnel	0	0	1	0	1	0	0	0
Reports of the Secretary-General on Sudan and South Sudan	23	13	19	1	20	1	1	0
Sierra Leone	0	6	0	0	1	0	0	0
Situation between Iraq and Kuwait	1	0	0	0	0	0	1	1
Small arms and light weapons	1	0	0	0	1	0	0	0
Somalia	8	7	8	5	8	7	0	0
Sudan	12	2	12	0	12	0	0	0
Sudan sanctions	1	0	1	0	0	0	0	0
Sudan and South Sudan	2	2	3	0	2	0	0	0
Threats to international peace and security caused by terrorist acts	1	0	1	0	0	0	9	4
Timor-Leste	2	0	0	0	1	2	0	0
UN peacekeeping operations	2	0	2	0	1	1	0	2
Women and peace and security	–	–	5	2	5	1	0	0

4.3.1 Protection of Civilians in Armed Conflict

The resolutions on the protection of civilians in armed conflict were first introduced in 1999[9] on ground of humanitarian concerns.[10] Aimed at protecting civilians as persons protected under international law,[11] this set of resolutions is regarded as a

[9]Res. 1265(1999).

[10]Res. 1265(1999), para. 10; Res. 1674(2006), para. 22; PRST/2010/25, para. 18 ('The Security Council emphasizes that all civilians affected by armed conflict, including those suffering losses as a result of lawful acts under international law, deserve assistance and recognition in respect of their inherent dignity as human beings').

[11]Res. 1296(2000), para. 3.

contribution towards the effective implementation of existing humanitarian law.[12] Resolution 1894(2009) states:

> [T]he Geneva Conventions of 1949… together with their Additional Protocols constitute the basis for the legal framework for the protection of civilians in armed conflict.[13]

The legal basis of the SC commitment to the protection of civilians in armed conflict[14] also includes other relevant international instruments such as the Hague Conventions (1899 and 1907), the UN Convention on the Rights of the Child (1989),[15] and the Convention on the Safety of United Nations ad Associated Personnel (1994).[16] Relevant SC decisions are mentioned along with primary sources of international law as well.[17] From this perspective, violations of relevant rules of applicable international humanitarian and human rights law appear to be the threshold of legitimacy for SC actions.[18] This seems to be confirmed by the explicit recognition that 'peace and security, development and human rights are the pillars of the United Nations system and the foundations for collective security and well-being.'[19]

Other factors contributing to exacerbate the negative impact of conflicts on civilians include the proliferation of arms, in particular small arms and light weapons,[20] and disarmament.[21] Accordingly, the SC notes that the implementation of relevant international instruments, such as the Convention on the Use, Stockpiling, Production and Transfer of Anti-Personnel Mines and Their Destruction (1997), may have beneficial effects on the safety of civilians.[22]

The considerations above suggest that this set of resolutions strongly contributes to strengthening existent international legal instruments. For example, the SC recognizes that one of the core challenges to the effective protection of civilians in armed conflict consists in enhancing compliance with international law.[23]

---

[12] Res. 1894(2009), para. 7(c).

[13] Res. 1894(2009), Preamble, para. 4.

[14] Res. 1296(2000), paras. 4 and 14–15; Res. 1738(2006), para. 4 (protection of journalists); Res. 1894(2009), Preamble, para. 1; Res. 1894(2009), para. 3.

[15] Res. 1265(1999), para. 4; and Res. 1738(2006), Preamble, para. 5.

[16] Res. 1265(1999), para. 9.

[17] Res. 1265(1999), para. 4; Res. 1674(2006), para. 6; Res. 1894(2009), para. 6.

[18] PRST/2013/2 para 9 ('The Council reaffirms its readiness to adopt appropriate measures aimed at those who violate international humanitarian and human rights law'). See also Res. 1674(2006), para. 5; Res. 1738(2006), para. 5; and Res. 1894(2009), para. 5 (reiterating its call on States that have not already done so to consider signing, ratifying or acceding to the relevant instruments of international humanitarian, human rights and refugee law). See also Res. 2175(2014), para. 1 (referring to the need to comply with international humanitarian, human rights and refugee law).

[19] Res. 1674(2006), Preamble, para. 3.

[20] Res. 1267(1999), para. 17; Res. 1674(2006), Preamble, para. 5; and Res. 1894(2009), para. 29.

[21] PRST/2004/46, paras. 6 and 10.

[22] Res. 1265(1999), para. 18 and Res. 1296(2000), paras. 20–21.

[23] Res. 1894(2009), Preamble, para. 19.

Accordingly, rules and principles of international law, the UN Charter and SC resolutions are often mentioned in the same provision and appear to stay on an equal footing.[24] However, the scrutinized SC decisions do not create new legal obligations beyond the SC commitment to the protection of civilians in armed conflict. What emerges from the text of SC resolutions and PRSTs under scrutiny is that international law is recognized as the benchmark of legitimacy of SC actions.[25] For example, a passage from resolution 1296(2000) reads:

> [The SC] Notes that the deliberate targeting of civilian populations or other protected persons and the committing of systematic, flagrant and widespread violations of international humanitarian and human rights law in situations of armed conflict may constitute a threat to international peace and security.[26]

In light of the preceding, the issue of the effectiveness of this set of resolutions turns out to be of paramount importance in determining whether international law is able to contain, wholly or partially, the discretionary powers of the SC. The progressive consideration by the SC of the protection of civilians as a thematic issue has led to the adoption of the Aide Memoire as a means to facilitate its consideration of issues pertaining to civilians.[27] The Preamble to the Fifth Edition (2014) reads:

> Enhancing the protection of civilians in armed conflict is at the core of the work of the United Nations Security Council for the maintenance of peace and security.[28]

Primarily aimed at facilitating SC deliberations on the establishment, change or close of peacekeeping operations,[29] the Aide Memoire may also provide guidance in circumstances outside the scope of peacekeeping operations which may require the urgent attention by the SC.[30] The document is based on the SC previous consideration of these issues and lists SC resolutions and PRSTs that make reference to such concerns.[31] However, the Preamble to the Aide Memoire provides that its adoption is without prejudice to the provisions of SC resolutions and other decisions.[32] Considering that the rationale behind SC interventions is represented

---

[24] Res. 1265(1999), para. 3; Res. 1296(2000), Preamble, para. 7; Res. 1894(2009), para. 1.

[25] Res. 1894(2009), para. 8. .

[26] Res. 1296(2000), para. 5. For similar expression of commitment, see Res. 1265(1999), para. 2; Res. 1674(2006), para. 26; Res. 1738(2006), Preamble, para. 6 ('Emphasizing that there are existing prohibitions under international humanitarian law against attacks intentionally directed against civilians, as such, which in situations of armed conflict constitute war crimes'); Res. 1738 (2006), para. 9; and Res. 1894(2009), paras. 2–3.

[27] PRST/2002/6, Annex (Aide Memoire); PRST/2002/41, para. 4; PRST/2003/27, para. 3; PRST/2004/46, para. 13 (describing the Aide Memoire as 'a practical tool').

[28] PRST 2014/3, Preamble, para. 1.

[29] Res. 1894(2009), para. 30.

[30] PRST/2002/6, Annex, paras. 4–5; PRST/2009/1, para. 8; PRST/2010/25, Annex, paras. 5 and 7; PRST/2013/2, para. 25; and PRST 2014/3, Annex Memoire, para. 5.

[31] PRST/2003/27, Annex, para, 4; and PRST 2014/3, Annex Memoire, para. 3.

[32] PRST/2002/6, Annex, para. 6; PRST/2003/27, Annex, para. 7; and PRST/2010/25, Annex, para. 4.

exclusively by violations of rules and principles of international law,[33] two issues emerge.

On one hand, Section F of the fifth edition of the Aide Memoire (2014) regulates the issue of compliance by parties to an armed conflict with applicable international humanitarian law and human rights law. Paragraph 2 thereof, in particular, explicitly recognizes the power of the SC to apply targeted sanctions against those parties that commit violations of applicable international humanitarian law and human rights law.[34] This, coupled with the request that all parties to a conflict strictly comply with international law and its resolutions on this matter,[35] suggests that if the SC acts as the guardian of the integrity of existent international law, it is not allowed to act in violation of those rules and principles.

On the other hand, however, the SC maintains that consideration of issues pertaining to the protection of civilians in armed conflict must be decided where appropriate and on a case-by-case basis,[36] taking into consideration the particular circumstances.[37] This leads to the awkward conclusion that while all actors involved in armed conflict are strictly bound to the obligations applicable to them under international law, the SC is legitimized to choose which situations address, and redress, for violations of international law. Beyond political considerations, this amounts to say that the SC is legitimized to inaction whenever convenience so suggests, overtly in violation of the spirit of the UN Charter and of its own resolutions. From this point of view, the SC resolutions on civilians are not able to qualify the discretionary powers of the SC, although they may exercise some influence over its politics.

4.3.2 *Women and Peace and Security*

The SC resolutions on women, peace and security are aimed at protecting women as a particularly vulnerable category of civilians in armed conflict.[38] Drawing on the assumption that there is an explicit connection between the protection of women's rights and maintenance of international peace and security,[39] the SC has repeatedly

[33]PRST/2008/18, para. 2 ('The Security Council condemns all violations of international law, including international humanitarian law, human rights law and refugee law committed against civilians in situations of armed conflict'); PRST/2010/25, para. 7; PRST/2013/2, para. 6; and 2014/3, para. 6.

[34]Res. 1265(1999), para. 16.

[35]PRST/2013/2, para. 7.

[36]Res. 1674(2006), para. 16; and PRST 2014/3, Annex Memoire, para. 4.

[37]PRST/2002/6, para. 3; PRST 2014/3, Annex Memoire, para. 5.

[38]Res. 1325(2000), Preamble, para. 4; Res. 2106(2013), para. 20; and Res. 2122(2013), Preamble, para. 7.

[39]Res. 1325(2000), Preamble, paras. 5 and 10; Res. 1820(2008), Preamble, para. 10; Res. 2122 (2013), Preamble, para. 4.

expressed its willingness to strengthen the role of women in the prevention and resolution of conflict, and in peacebuilding operations.[40]

The commitment of the SC is articulated into three action points. The first one consists of the endorsement of a set of international norms to which all parties to an armed conflict should conform. They include the Geneva Conventions (1949) and the Additional Protocols thereto (1977), the Refugee Convention (1951) and the Protocol thereto (1967), the Convention on the Elimination of All Forms of Discrimination against Women (1979) and the Optional Protocol thereto (1999), the Convention on the Rights of the Child (1989) and the Optional Protocols thereto (2000) as well as the relevant provisions of the Statute of the International Criminal Court.[41]

The second one is represented by the SC willingness to assess the impact of measures adopted under Article 41 of the UN Charter on women, in order to consider appropriate humanitarian exemptions.[42]

The third one consists of the adoption of a gender perspective into peacekeeping and peacebuilding operations, including providing training on the protection, rights and particular needs of women to UN personnel involved in peacekeeping and post-conflict operations.[43]

It seems that this set of resolutions recognizes relevant international humanitarian and human rights law as the standard of legality against which to assess the legality of actions taken by the parties to an armed conflict.[44] Violations of such provisions can therefore be regarded as the threshold for considering a given

[40]Res. 1888(2009), Preamble, paras. 1 and 22; Res. 1889(2009), Preamble, para. 1; Res. 1960 (2010), Preamble, para. 1; Res. 2106(2013), Preamble, paras. 1 and 3; and Res. 2122(2013), Preamble, para 1.

[41]Res. 1325(2000), para. 9; Res. 1820(2008), Preamble, paras. 5 and 9; Res. 1888(2009), Preamble, para. 5; Res. 1888(2009), Preamble, para. 9; Res. 1889(2009), Preamble, para. 3; Res. 1960(2010), Preamble, para. 12; Res. 2106(2013), Preamble, para. 9; Res. 2122(2013), Preamble, para. 2. Other documents include the World Summit Outcome document (2005) and the Beijing Declaration and Platform for Action (1995), as reported in Res. 1820(2008), Preamble, paras. 3–4; Res. 1888(2009), Preamble, para. 4; Res. 1889(2009), Preamble, para. 3; and Res. 2122(2013), Preamble, para. 2.

[42]Res. 1325(2000), para. 14; Res. 1889(2009), para. 5. See also Res. 1888(2009), para. 10; Res. 1960(2010), para. 7; and Res. 2106(2013), para. 13.

[43]Res. 1325(2000), paras. 1–8; Res. 1888(2009), paras. 11–12; Res. 1960(2010), paras. 11 and 16.

[44]Res. 1820(2008), Preamble, para. 12; Res. 1960(2010), Preamble, para. 8; Res. 2106(2013), Preamble, para. 7; and Res. 2122(2013), Preamble, para. 10 ('Recognizing that States bear primary responsibility to respect and ensure the human rights of their citizens, as well as all individuals within their territory as provided for by relevant international law'); Res. 1888(2009), Preamble, paras. 10; and Res. 1960(2010), Preamble, paras. 4 ('Stressing the necessity for all States and non-States parties to conflicts to comply fully with their obligations under applicable international law, including the prohibition on all forms of sexual violence'), and 6–7; Res. 1889(2009), para. 5 ('[The SC] Reiterates its call for all parties in armed conflicts to respect fully international law applicable to the rights and protection of women and girls'); Res. 1960(2010), Preamble, para. 9; Res. 2106(2013), Preamble, paras. 11–12, and para. 2 (operative part); and Res. 2122(2013), Preamble, para. 10, and 13.

situation as a threat, actual or potential, to international peace and security which justifies SC actions. For instance, the SC recognizes that:

> [R]ape and other forms of sexual violence can constitute a war crime, a crime against humanity, or a constitutive act with respect to genocide [...]
> [The SC] Affirms its intention, when establishing and renewing state-specific sanctions regimes, to take into consideration the appropriateness of targeted and graduated measures against parties to situations of armed conflict who commit rape and other forms of sexual violence against women and girls in situations of armed conflict.'[45]

From this perspective, the SC intervention draws legitimacy from applicable international law. In light of the aim of the SC resolutions on women,[46] a passage from resolution 1888(2009) appears to confirm this conclusion: '[The SC recalls] that international humanitarian law affords general protection to women and children as part of the civilian population during armed conflicts and special protection due to the fact that they can be placed particularly at risk.'[47] This further suggests that, in theory, this set of resolutions strengthens and complements existent provisions of international legal instruments. In practice, however, the effectiveness of the above-mentioned resolutions—that is to say, the extent to which, if any, they are able to restrain the discretionary powers bestowed by the UN Charter on the SC—is contested.

On one hand, the SC has expressed its willingness to promote the implementation of its resolutions on women through active cooperation with the Economic and Social Council (ECOSOC) and the General Assembly[48] as well as the Secretary-General.[49] It also acknowledges that 'armed and other types of conflicts still persist in many parts of the world and are an ongoing reality affecting women in nearly every region.'[50] This is further confirmed by the recognition that brutal acts of violence against women, especially sexual violence, in situations of armed conflict 'in some situations have become systematic and widespread.'[51]

On the other hand, the willingness of the SC to address those situations is limited to situations already on the agenda of the SC.[52] However, recent studies have shown that the powers of the SC are characterized by an inherent tension between compliance with the terms of its mandate and a degree of discretion related to the

[45]Res. 1820(2008), paras. 4–5. See also Res. 1889(2009), para. 3.

[46]See note 38 above.

[47]Res. 1888(2009), Preamble, para. 6.

[48]PRST/2004/40, para. 10.

[49]PRST/2006/42, para. 14; PRST/2007/40, para. 9.

[50]PRST/2007/40, para. 5. See also Res. 1960(2010), Preamble, para. 2 ('as documented in the Secretary-General's report').

[51]Res. 1820(2008), Preamble, para. 8; and Res. 1888(2009), Preamble, para. 3.

[52]Res. 1960(2010), para. 1. This limit in scope of the SC commitment is reiterated in the request to the Secretary-General to include in his annual report a list of 'the parties that are credibly suspected of committing or being responsible for patterns of sexual violence in situations of armed conflict on the Security Council agenda,' which will be used 'as a basis for [taking] measures in accordance with the procedures of the relevant sanctions committees.' Res. 1960(2010), para. 3.

selection of the actions (or inactions) taken, which ultimately amounts to a biased compliance with the UN Charter obligations.[53] In particular, existent studies show that the actions taken by the SC in the last decade disproportionately target conflicts taking place in Africa and the Middle East,[54] a situation which may affect the impartiality of the politics of the SC in relation to the protection of the rights of women in armed conflict. This suggests that the subsequent intention of the SC to take action on a comprehensive set of indicators to track implementation of SC resolution 1325(2000)[55] and to strengthen its commitment[56] is sensibly devalued.

4.3.3 Children in Armed Conflict

The resolutions on children and armed conflict establish the threshold of legality of SC actions whenever instances of targeting of children by parties to an armed conflict or their use as soldiers happen.[57] The normative foundations of this set of resolutions are entirely based on international treaties, such as the International Labour Organization Convention No. 182 on the Prohibition and Immediate Action for the Elimination of the Worst Forms of Child Labor and the provisions of the Statute of the International Criminal Court characterizing the use of child soldiers as a war crime.[58] The range of issues covered by this set of resolutions also extends to include the linkages between the illicit traffic of small arms and light weapons and armed conflict, with a view to addressing its impact on children.[59] Thus, the Ottawa Convention on the Prohibition of the Use, Stockpiling, Production and Transfer of Anti-Personnel Mines and on Their Destruction, for instance, is regarded as an integral part of the legal basis of SC resolutions on children.[60]

Subsequent SC intervention has a humanitarian character, which is manifested by the request, formulated in absolute terms, that all parties to an armed conflict strictly comply with the four Geneva Conventions (1949), the Convention on the

---

[53]Deplano (2014), Vargiu and Deplano (2014).

[54]Deplano (2014), Vargiu and Deplano (2014).

[55]PRST/2010/8, para. 6; PRST/2010/22, paras. 10 and 12; and PRST 2014/21, para. 12.

[56]Res. 2122(2013), paras. 3 and 17.

[57]Res. 1460(2003), Preamble, para. 1 (recognizing that SC resolutions on children and armed conflict 'provide a comprehensive framework for addressing the protection of children affected by armed conflict'); Res. 1612(2005), Preamble, para. 5; Res. 2143(2014), Preamble, para. 1.

[58]Res. 1261(1999), Preamble, para. 2; and Res. 1539(2004), Preamble, para. 7.

[59]Res. 1612(2005), Preamble, para. 9.

[60]Res. 1314(2000), Preamble, paras. 5, and 8 (operative part). Other recognized linkages include armed conflict and terrorism, the illicit trade in precious minerals, and other criminal activities which can prolong or intensify their impact on children. See Res. 1379(2001), para. 6; and Res. 1539(2004), para. 3.

Rights of the Child (1988) and Protocols thereto.[61] Moreover, the text of resolutions provides details of the commitment of the SC itself to the protection, welfare and rights of children in situations of armed conflict when considering the matters of which it is seized.[62] Such commitment consists of provision of humanitarian assistance to civilian populations in distress, including the protection of displaced children, and the willingness of the SC to give consideration to the potential unintended consequences of sanctions adopted under Article 41 of the UN Charter, in order to consider appropriate humanitarian exemptions that take into account children's specific needs.[63]

It appears that this multi-faceted, self-imposed duty on part of the SC is subordinated to international law. For example, paragraph 18 of SC resolution 1261 (1999) reads:

> [The SC] reaffirms also its readiness to consider appropriate responses whenever buildings or sites which usually have a significant presence of children are specifically targeted in situations of armed conflict, in violation of international law.

Provisions of this kind[64] must be read in conjunction with the SC's commitment to support 'the Secretary-General's call for "an era of application" of international norms and standards for the protection of children affected by armed conflict.'[65]

Overall, this set of resolutions strengthens and complements existent provisions of international law by conforming SC practice to international standards that have become customary international law, such as the provisions of the Geneva Conventions (1949). However, with regard to the effectiveness of these resolutions as restraint to the discretionary powers of the SC, it seems that neither the set of resolutions on children and armed conflict themselves nor the international legal

---

[61]Res. 1261(1999), para. 3; Res. 1314(2000), para. 3; Res. 1379(2001), para. 8(a); Res. 1539(2004), Preamble, para. 7; Res. 1882(2009), Preamble, para. 8; Res. 2143(2014), Preamble, para. 4. See also PRST/2008/6, para. 5 (referring to the principles of humanity, neutrality, impartiality and independence).

[62]Res. 1314(2000), para. 9; Res. 1379(2001), para. 1; PRST/2002/12, para. 1 ('The Security Council… expresses its commitment to the protection of children affected by armed conflict as an essential component of its work to promote and maintain international peace and security'); Res. 1460(2003), Preamble, para. 3; Res. 1539(2004), Preamble, paras. 5 and 8; Res. 1612(2005), Preamble, para. 6; Res. 1882(2009), Preamble, para. 9, and 7 (operative part); Res. 1998(2011), Preamble, para. 2; and Res. 2068(2012), Preamble, para. 2.

[63]Res. 1261(1999), paras. 16–17; Res. 1314(2000), para. 15; Res. 1379(2001), para. 7; Res. 1998 (2011), para. 9; and Res. 2068(2012), para. 3(b).

[64]Other provisions referring to provisions of international law relating to the rights and protection of children in armed conflict as the parameter of legality for SC actions include Res. 1379(2001), para. 9(b-c); Res. 1460(2003), paras. 7–8; Res. 1539(2004), Preamble, para. 3; Res. 1539(2004), para. 5; Res. 1612(2005), Preamble paras 2 and 7; Res. 1882(2009), Preamble, para. 10; PRST/2009/9, paras. 5, 10, and 15 ('The Security Council also urges parties to armed conflict to refrain from actions that impede children's access to education, in particular attacks or threats of attack on school children or teachers as such, the use of schools for military operations, and attacks on schools that are prohibited by applicable international law'); and Res. 1998(2011), para. 4.

[65]Res. 1460(2003), para. 1.

instruments referred to therein are able to oblige the SC to consider any situation of armed conflict as a threat to or breach of international peace and security, and possibly act upon it. The case of the creation of a UN-wide monitoring and reporting system, which culminated with the creation of the Security Council Working Group on Children and Armed Conflict,[66] is exemplificative.

By providing that 'the implementation of the monitoring and reporting mechanism by the Secretary-General will be undertaken only in the context of and for the specific purpose of ensuring the protection of children affected by armed conflict and *shall not thereby prejudge or imply a decision by the Security Council as to whether or not to include a situation on its agenda*,'[67] it seems that the SC has potentially legitimized itself to discriminate which children's human rights violations occurring at the same time throughout the world are worth protecting and which ones are not. This conclusion is further strengthened by the consideration that the purpose of establishing the monitoring mechanism is 'to collect and provide timely, objective, accurate and reliable information on the recruitment and use of child soldiers in violation of applicable international law and on other violations and abuses committed against children affected by armed conflict, and the mechanism will report to the working group to be created in accordance with paragraph 8 of [resolution 1612(2005)].'[68] However, since the SC Working Group is composed of all SC members, the impartiality of the monitoring and reporting mechanism results unambiguously affected.

4.3.4 International Terrorism

The first resolution to address the issue of international terrorism traces back to the end of the twentieth century. The resolution declared that acts of international terrorism have a damaging effect on international relations and jeopardize the security of states.[69] It also stressed the determination of the international community to eliminate all forms of international terrorism[70] and clarified that actions taken by the members of the SC must conform to the provisions of the UN Charter and international law.[71] Accordingly, it called upon all States to adopt effective and practical measures for security cooperation, in compliance with international law.[72]

---

[66] Res. 1612(2005), para. 2.

[67] Emphasis added. See also Res. 1612(2005), para. 4; Res. 1882(2009), paras. 2, 10 and 19(a); Res. 1998(2011), para. 2; and Res. 1998(2011), para. 2.

[68] Res. 1612(2005), para. 2(a).

[69] Res. 1189(1998), Preamble, paras. 2–3.

[70] Res. 1189(1998), Preamble, paras. 3 and 7.

[71] PRST S/23500, para. 11.

[72] Res. 1189(1998), para. 5.

However, in the aftermath of the 9/11 attacks, the SC decided to fully regulate the practical measures for security cooperation referred to in previous resolutions by imposing a top-down, homogeneous strategy to the international community as a whole. Such strategy includes the task of tracking progress of compliance with its resolutions as well.[73]

The resolutions on international terrorism comprise four groups resolutions—namely, those on International terrorism, Threats to international peace and security caused by terrorist acts, Threats to international peace and security: Security Council Summit (2005) and Threats to international peace and security.[74] They seem to establish the legal basis of SC action in this field, the limits to the use of its discretionary powers and the actions to be taken by all states in order to ensure full implementation of the relevant SC resolutions.[75]

Thus, on one hand the SC maintains that 'acts, methods and practices of terrorism are contrary to the purposes and principles of the United Nations, including 'knowingly financing, planning and inciting terrorist acts,'[76] since they 'endanger innocent lives and the dignity and security of human beings everywhere, threaten the social and economic development of all states and undermine global stability and prosperity.'[77] As such, they constitute a threat to international peace and security[78] and fall within the purview of the SC's responsibility.[79] In this respect, the SC

[73]See Res. 1368(2001) and following ones.

[74]Res. 1189(1998) (international terrorism); Res. 2178(2014) and previous one (threats to international peace and security caused by terrorist acts); Res. 1625(2005) and previous one (threats to international peace and security: Security Council Summit 2005); and Res. 2195(2014) and previous one (threats to international peace and security).

[75]Contrary to the other thematic resolutions, some of the resolutions on international terrorism have been adopted under Chapter VII of the UN Charter. They include: Res. 1373(2001); Res. 1452(2002); Res. 1455(2003); Res. 1526(2004); Res. 1566(2004); Res. 1617(2005); Res. 1735 (2006); Res. 1822(2005); Res. 1904(2009); Res. 1988(2011); Res. 1989(2011); Res. 2082(2012); Res. 2083(2012); Res. 2160(2014); Res. 2161(2014); Res. 2170(2014); and Res. 2178(2014).

[76]Res. 1373(2001), paras. 5 and 6 (stressing that acts of terrorism are motivated by intolerance or extremism). See also Res. 1624(2005), Preamble, para. 8 and Res. 2133(2014), Preamble, paras. 1 and 13.

[77]Res. 1377(2001), Annex, para. 7. See also Res. 1566(2004), Preamble, para. 8 and Res. 2129 (2013), Preamble, para. 8 (stressing that 'acts of terrorism seriously impair the enjoyment of human rights and threaten the social and economic development of all States and undermine global stability and prosperity).

[78]Res. 1373(2001), Preamble, para. 3; Res. 1455(2003), Preamble, para. 7; Res. 1535(2004), Preamble, para. 2; Res. 1566(2004), Preamble, para. 7; Res. 1617(2005), Preamble, para. 2; Res. 1618(2005), para. 1; Res. 1787(2007), Preamble, para. 2; Res. 1805(2008), Preamble, para. 1; Res. 1822(2008), Preamble, para. 2; Res. 1904(2009), Preamble, para. 2; Res. 1989(2011), Preamble, para. 2; Res. 2083(2012), Preamble, para. 2; Res. 2129(2013), Preamble, para. 1; Res. 2133(2014), Preamble, para. 1; Res. 2161(2014), Preamble, para. 2; Res. 2170(2014), Preamble, para. 3; Res. 2178(2014), Preamble, para. 1; and Res. 2195(2014), Preamble, para. 2.

[79]Res. 1373(2001), para. 8; Res. 1438(2002), para. 4; Res. 1440(2002), para. 5; Res. 1450(2002), Preamble, para. 1; Res. 1465(2003), para. 4; Res. 1516(2003), para. 4; and Res. 1535(2004), Preamble, para. 3.

recognizes that there is a direct link between drug trafficking and international terrorism since the use of proceeds derived from illicit cultivation, production and trafficking of narcotic drugs and their precursors constitutes a form of financing or support of terrorist activities.[80] Accordingly, it has repeatedly called on states to comply with or ratify relevant conventions and protocols, including the Single Convention on Narcotic Drugs (1961) and related Protocol (1972), the Convention on Psychotropic Substances (1971), the UN Convention against Transnational Organized Crime (2000) and Protocols thereto, and the UN Convention against Corruption (2003).[81]

Acts of terrorism also justify the exercise of the inherent right of individual or collective self-defence, as recognized by the UN Charter.[82] From a pure pragmatic point of view, the SC also recognizes that combating international terrorism requires a collective, concerted effort of the international community:

> Terrorism can only be defeated by a sustained and comprehensive approach involving the active participation and collaboration of all States, and international and regional organizations to impede, impair, isolate, and incapacitate the terrorist threat.[83]

On the other hand, the SC decided to take control of the strategy for combating international terrorism by requiring states to fully implement its resolutions. Two elements characterize the new SC-guided form of international cooperation in the field of international security.

The first element is the systematic reference to international law,[84] including applicable international human rights, refugee, and humanitarian law,[85] and the purposes and principles of the UN Charter[86] as the threshold of legality of both SC and states' actions. A passage from resolution 1535(2004) reads:

---

[80]Res. 1988(2011), para. 5 and Res. 2082(2012), Preamble, para. 4 (referring to the situation in Afghanistan). Other related activities include proliferation of weapons of mass destruction, small arms and light weapons, transnational organized crime, piracy and human trafficking; see Res. 2160(2014), Preamble, para. 3 and Res. 2195(2014), Preamble, para. 7.

[81]Res. 2195(2014), para. 3.

[82]Res. 1368(2001), Preamble, para. 3 and Res. 1373(2001), Preamble, para. 4.

[83]Res. 1735(2006), Preamble, para. 5. See also Res. 1822(2008), Preamble, para. 8 and Res. 1904 (2009), Preamble, para. 6; Res. 1989(2011), Preamble, para. 7; Res. 2083(2012), Preamble, para. 7; Res. 2161(2014), Preamble, para. 7; and Res. 2195(2014), Preamble, para. 4.

[84]Res. 1373(2001), para. 3; Res. 1377(2001), Annex, para. 8; Res. 1455(2003), Preamble, para. 3; Res. 1526(2004), Preamble, para. 3; Res. 1566(2004), Preamble, para. 3, and para 1 (operative part); Res. 1617(2005), Preamble, para. 4.

[85]Res. 1822(2008), Preamble, para. 3; Res. 1988(2011), Preamble, para. 8; Res. 1989(2011), Preamble, para. 5; Res. 2082(2012), Preamble, para. 8; Res. 2083(2012), Preamble, para. 5; Res. 2160(2014), Preamble, para. 8; Res. 2161(2014), Preamble, para. 5; Res. 2170(2014), Preamble, para. 17; and Res. 2195(2014), Preamble, para. 20.

[86]Res. 1368(2001), Preamble, para. 1; Res. 1373(2001), Preamble, para. 5; Res. 1377(2001), Annex, para. 8; Res. 1438(2002), Preamble, para. 2; Res. 1625(2005), Annex, Preamble, para. 2; Res. 2170(2014), Preamble, para. 2.

> [States] must ensure that any measure to combat terrorism comply with all their obligations under international law, and should adopt such measures in accordance with international law, in particular international human rights law, refugee, and humanitarian law.[87]

Sometimes the resolutions of the SC are mentioned together with the purposes and principles of the UN Charter and appear to be on an equal footing.[88] In line with this, relevant resolutions contain several calls on states to implement existing anti-terrorist conventions[89] (and SC resolutions).[90] This aspect of the SC resolutions on international terrorism appears to strengthen the view that this group of thematic resolutions effectively contribute to the development of international law through the crystallization of existent rules of international law.

The second element is represented by the detailed instructions imparted by the SC to member states. They are usually phrased in the form of peremptory provisions recognised as legislative powers and focus on ensuring that all states have legislation in place covering all aspects of resolution 1373(2001),[91] which is regarded as having a special nature.[92] To monitor compliance with its resolutions, the SC has established an ad hoc Counter-Terrorism Committee and Sanctions Committee in accordance with rule 28 of its rules of procedure.[93]

It is peculiar that among the resolutions on international terrorism, four of them stand out as being directed to a specific country rather than the international community as a whole[94] and, significantly, have been adopted under Chapter VII of the UN Charter. This can be interpreted as a sign of selection bias against a specific geographical region. However, this is also a demonstration that there exists a direct, explicit link between selection bias and the development of certain areas of international law.[95]

---

[87] Res. 1535(2004), Preamble, para. 4. An identical provision is contained in Res. 1566(2004), Preamble, para. 6; Res. 1624(2005), Preamble, para. 2; and Res. 1787(2007), Preamble, para 4; Res. 1805(2008), Preamble, para. 8; Res. 1904(2009), Preamble, para. 3; Res. 2129(2013), Preamble, para. 5; Res. 2133(2014), Preamble, para. 8; Res. 2170(2014), Preamble, para. 8; Res. 2178(2014), Preamble, para. 7 (also stressing that failure to comply with international obligations is one of the factors contributing to increased radicalization and fosters a sense of impunity).

[88] Res. 1438(2002), Preamble, para. 1; Res. 1440(2002), Preamble, para. 1; Res. 1450(2002), Preamble, para. 1; Res. 1465(2003), Preamble, para. 1; Res. 1516(2003), Preamble, para. 1; Res. 1530(2004), Preamble, para. 1; Res. 1611(2005), Preamble, para. 1; and Res. 1618(2005), Preamble, para. 3.

[89] Res. 1368(2001), para. 4; Res. 1373(2001), Preamble, para. 7; Res. 1377(2001), Annex, para. 10; Res. 1450(2002), Preamble, para. 2; Res. 1535(2004), Preamble, para. 5; Res. 1566(2004), paras. 4–5; Res. 1624(2005), Preamble, para. 11; Res. 2129(2013), Preamble, para. 27; Res. 2133 (2014), Preamble, para. 4; and Res. 2178(2014), Preamble, para. 21.

[90] Res. 1368(2001), para. 4.

[91] Res. 1452(2002), paras. 1–4; Res. 1455(2003), Preamble, para. 2; and Res. 1526(2004), Preamble, para. 2.

[92] Res. 1535(2004), Preamble, para. 15.

[93] Res. 1373(2001), para. 6; and Res. 1988(2011), para. 30.

[94] Res. 1988(2011), para. 5; Res. 2082(2012) and Res. 2160(2014) on Afghanistan; Res. 2170 (2014) on Syria.

[95] This issue is further explored in Chap. 5.

4.4 Beyond Implied Powers: Thematic Resolutions as Self-Imposed Duties

In the absence of a definition of international peace and security, it appears that the expansion of the SC mandate in the form of adoption of thematic resolutions is not against the provisions of the UN Charter. Accordingly, thematic resolutions, especially those adopted under Chapter VII of the UN Charter, cannot be regarded as *ultra vires*. Likewise, they do not appear to fall within the traditional understanding of implied powers[96] so long as their main effect can be quantified in terms of contributions of individual resolutions to the crystallization or development of international law. In that sense, in as much as the actions of the SC are subordinated to general international law, the substantive law recalled in thematic resolutions—especially those on women, children and civilians—automatically becomes a formal limit to SC action.

From this perspective, thematic resolutions may be regarded as a peculiar instance of the discretionary powers of the SC, in the sense that as long as they contribute to the development of international law they generate a cascade effect whose repercussions equally affect acts of member states implementing SC resolutions and the SC alike. Tellingly, the resolutions on women, children, civilians and international terrorism have become increasingly cited in other thematic and non-thematic resolutions, signifying that a hardening process of certain rules of international law, especially in the fields of international humanitarian and human rights law,[97] is taking place.

In this context, it is significant that the resolutions on Mali refer in equal measure to the resolutions on the protection of civilians, women and children in the dispositive part of the resolution rather than in the Preamble, which contains only statements of principle. They also acknowledge the fundamental importance of the resolutions on international terrorism in both the Preamble and the operative part of the text of resolutions. This attitude of the SC towards the thematic resolutions can be seen as a testimony to the relevance and, in varying degrees, the legally binding force of general international law on state and non-state actors alike.

However, the real impact of the thematic resolutions on the powers of the SC is rather limited due to the fact that re-cited resolutions in general do not constitute a precedent and, accordingly, the SC can depart from them, entirely or partially, without being in breach of any rule of international law. Furthermore, the content of thematic resolutions is not static and can be updated and modified by the SC at any time. The fact that the adoption of thematic resolutions and the constant reference to them in non-thematic resolution has become a recurrent pattern in SC practice can nonetheless be seen as an uncontroversial sign of commitment of the SC towards upholding the international rule of law as the main factor contributing to the maintenance of international peace and security.

---

[96]As discussed in Chap. 2, Sect. 2.3.

[97]See Chap. 5, Sect. 5.3.

4.5 Conclusion

This chapter has provided an overview of the thematic resolutions adopted by the SC since 1946, with a focus on those on women, children and civilians on one hand, and those on international terrorism on the other hand. The findings of the analysis show that while the SC maintains a great deal of leeway in deciding when, and in respect to whom, to take action, it has developed a new pattern of resolutions that eventually contain self-imposed duties, in addition to the formal limits as to the scope of its mandate set forth in the UN Charter. Despite much reference to general international law as the backbone of the benchmark of legality of all international actors including, to a certain extent, the SC, the presence of selection bias in the behavioural patterns of the SC raises suspicion about the genuine and full commitment of the SC to those rules and principles.

Bibliography

Deplano, Rossana. 2014. Building a taxonomy of UN Security Council decisions: A biased compliance with the UN Charter obligations? *State Practice and International Law Journal* 1: 139–160.

Reisman, Michel W. 1993. The constitutional crisis in the United Nations. *American Journal of International Law* 87: 83–100.

Vargiu, Paolo, and Deplano, Rossana. 2014. The human rights dimension of UN Security Council resolutions. In *Essays on human rights: A celebration of the life of Dr. Janusz Kochanowski*, ed. Jo Carby-Hall, 520–541. Warsaw: Ius et Lex.

Chapter 5
Security Council Resolutions and Selection Bias

5.1 Introduction

This chapter aims to establish whether the proclaimed Security Council (SC) commitment to upholding relevant international law is tainted by appearance of bias. To that end, it creates a taxonomy of SC decisions in which resolutions are classified into three categories—namely, resolutions on geopolitical regions, thematic resolutions and a residual category of resolutions. Although many alternative perspectives can be used to establish whether the adopted resolutions are charged of bias, this chapter evaluates the internal coherence of SC resolutions by analysing the amount of international legal instruments cited in the text of resolutions. The underlying assumption is that the more international instruments are cited in the text of resolutions, the more unbiased are the SC resolutions adopted. An argument is made that there is an inherent tension between compliance with the terms of the SC mandate and a degree of discretion related to the selection of the subject-matters of resolutions, and such tension seems unavoidable. The chapter concludes with an assessment of the implications of current SC practice for the development of international law and proposes ways to reduce as much as possible the discretion in the hands of the SC in light of the purposes and principles of the UN Charter, which are often advocated in the text of SC resolutions.

5.2 Taxonomy of Security Council Resolutions: A Biased Compliance with the UN Charter Obligations?

The previous chapters have examined the normative context regulating the functioning of the SC and have subsequently discussed the extent to which international law is able to shape SC behavioral patterns with a view to finding coherence between theory and practice of SC powers. This section aims to establish whether

R. Deplano, *The Strategic Use of International Law by the United Nations Security Council*, SpringerBriefs in Law, DOI 10.1007/978-3-319-21281-4_5

the proclaimed SC commitment to upholding applicable international law is tainted by appearance of bias. To that end, it creates a taxonomy of the SC decisions adopted in the period of time between 1946 and 2014 with a view to finding selection effects. The empirical analysis is based on simple statistics and is carried out in relation to each of the three periods of time identified in Chap. 3—namely, origins and cold war period, post-cold war period and the twenty-first century.

As an introductory note to the analysis, it is worthy to point out here that from 1946 to 2014, the SC has adopted an average of 31.8 resolutions per year. However, the disaggregated data reveals that during the cold war period the average of resolutions per year is 15.8 while during the post-cold war period is 60.8. The figure further increases in the twenty-first century period, where the number of resolutions adopted on average each year reaches a staggering 86. The numbers highlight a trend in SC practice which is reflected in the progressive expansion of the SC mandate.

5.3 Origins and Cold War Period

In the period from 1946 to 1991, the SC adopted 725 resolutions. Grouped by categories of actions, the aggregated data shows that 77 % of resolutions address issues with a regional scope while 2 % of decisions address thematic issues. The remaining decisions—comprising 21 %, include actions previously agreed upon or taken by the broader family of UN institutions and seconded by the SC (see Fig. 5.1).

The disaggregated data in the geopolitical section further demonstrates that 238 resolutions—comprising 42 %, concern the Middle East region while 146 resolutions—comprising 26 % of all SC decisions, concern the African continent. Taken together, the number of SC decisions addressing issues taking place in Africa and the Middle East is equal to 384 out of 557—comprising 68 % of SC resolutions on geopolitical regions. The figures do not take into consideration any decision addressing UN activities in those geopolitical areas (which have been classified as 'UN/Other' related issues), but only actions taken by the SC (see Table 5.1).

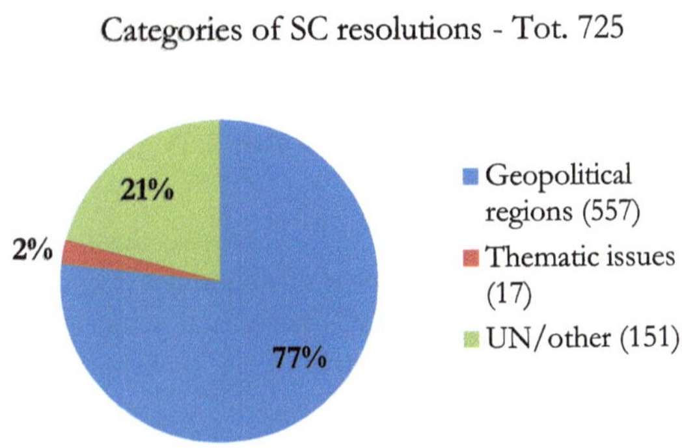

Fig. 5.1 Origins and cold war period (1946–1991)—aggregated data

Table 5.1 Disaggregated data on composition of resolutions on geopolitical regions (1946–1991)

Geopolitical region	No. of resolutions
Africa	146 (26 %)
Middle East	238 (42 %)
Europe	97 (18 %)
Other regions	76 (14 %)
Total	557 (100 %)

The composition of SC resolutions in the selected period of time suggests that, as long as the vast majority of resolutions address country-specific issues in two well-defined geopolitical areas, this could be interpreted as appearance of bias.

5.4 Post-cold War Period

In the period from 1992 to 2000, the SC adopted 608 resolutions. Grouped by categories of actions, the aggregated data shows that 75 % of resolutions address issues with a regional scope while 2 % of decisions address thematic issues. The remaining decisions—comprising 23 %, include actions previously agreed upon or taken by the broader family of UN institutions and seconded by the SC (see Fig. 5.2).

The disaggregated data in the geopolitical section further demonstrates that 180 resolutions—comprising 39 %, concern the African continent while 148 resolutions—comprising 32 % concern Europe. Furthermore, the results show that 77 resolutions—comprising 17 % of resolutions, concern the Middle East region. Taken together, the number of SC decisions addressing issues taking place in Africa and the Middle East is equal to 257 out of 459—comprising 56 % of SC resolutions on geopolitical regions. As in the figures for the cold war period, the computation does not take into consideration any decision addressing UN activities in those geopolitical areas (which have been classified as 'UN/Other' related issues), but only actions taken by the SC (see Table 5.2).

Fig. 5.2 Post-cold war period (1992–2000)—aggregated data

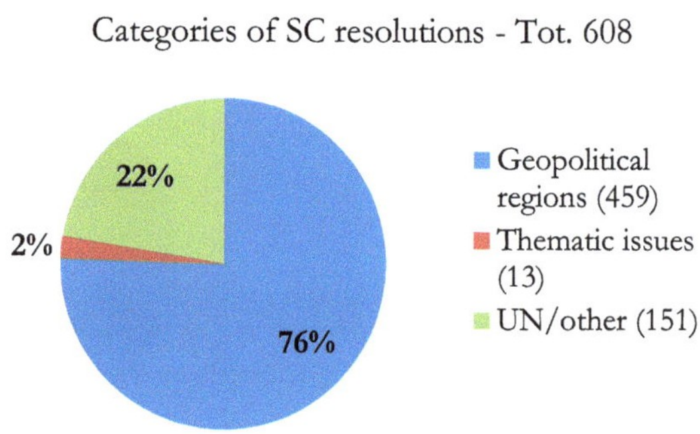

Table 5.2 Disaggregated data on composition of resolutions on geopolitical regions (1992–2000)

Geopolitical region	No. of resolutions
Africa	180 (39 %)
Middle East	77 (17 %)
Europe	148 (32 %)
Other regions	54 (12 %)
Total	459 (100 %)

The analysis above shows that the composition of SC resolutions adopted during the post-cold war period is homogeneous to the one of the resolutions adopted during the cold war period. However, the total of resolutions on Africa and the Middle East adopted between 1992 and 2000 drops from 68 % in the cold war period to 56 % whereas the resolutions on Europe witness a rising of 14 %, from 18 % in the cold war period to 32 %. Within the disaggregated data, it is significant that the resolutions on the Middle East, which scored highest in this category during the cold war period, went significantly down in the same proportion as the increase of resolutions on Africa. This suggests that there is no open evidence of selection bias in the post-cold war period resolutions, a presumption that is corroborated by the limited similarity with the composition of resolutions on geopolitical regions adopted between 1946 and 1991.

5.5 The Twenty-First Century

In the period from 2001 to 2014, the SC adopted 861 resolutions. Grouped by categories of actions, the aggregated data shows that 81 % of resolutions address issues with a regional scope while 10 % of decisions address thematic issues. The remaining decisions—comprising 9 %, include actions previously agreed upon or taken by the broader family of UN institutions and seconded by the SC (see Fig. 5.3).

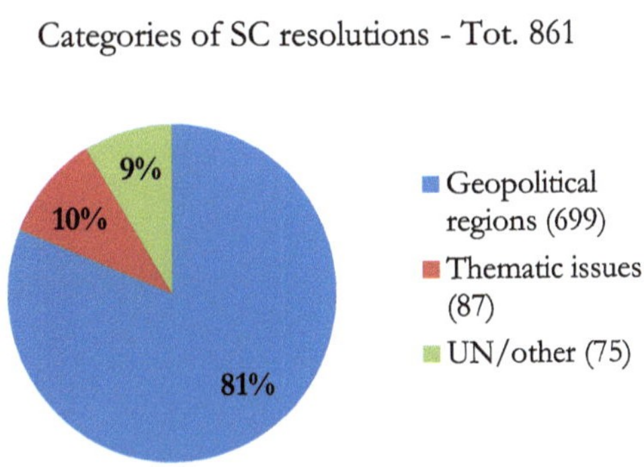

Fig. 5.3 The twenty-first century period (2001–2014)—aggregated data

Table 5.3 Disaggregated data on composition of resolutions on geopolitical regions (2001–2014)

Geopolitical region	No. of resolutions
Africa	417 (60 %)
Middle East	154 (22 %)
Europe	76 (11 %)
Other regions	52 (7 %)
Total	699 (100 %)

The disaggregated data in the geopolitical section further demonstrates that 417 resolutions—comprising 60 %, concern the African continent while 154 resolutions—comprising 22 % concern the Middle East region. Taken together, the number of SC decisions addressing issues taking place in Africa and the Middle East is equal to 571 out of 699—comprising 82 % of SC resolutions on geopolitical regions. As in the analysis of previous periods period, the figures do not take into consideration any decision addressing UN activities in those geopolitical areas (which have been classified as 'UN/Other' related issues), but only actions taken by the SC (see Table 5.3).

The analysis above shows that in the period of time between 2001 and 2014 the proportion of categories of resolutions significantly changed compared with the previous period. In particular, whether the increase of the number of resolutions addressing country-specific issues is proportional to the higher number of resolutions adopted, thematic resolutions have risen fivefold while the number of resolutions authorizing or seconding UN activities is halved. Figure 5.4 shows the disaggregated data of the twenty-first century resolutions.

The figures show that the number of resolutions adopted on Africa is equal to 48 % of all resolutions adopted between 2001 and 2014. Compared to the resolutions on the same subject-matter adopted in the previous two periods, it becomes apparent that the SC is devoting a substantial amount of attention to threats to international peace and security taking place in the African continent. The data in itself is not indicative of any behavioural pattern. However, it assumes a different weight when read in light of the corresponding figures in the previous periods of time: during the cold war period resolutions on Africa amounted to 26 % of the resolutions on geopolitical regions while during post-cold war period the figure went up to 39 %. The fact that in the twenty-first century has reached the peak of 60 % of resolutions on geopolitical regions signals a strong appearance of bias.

The presumption of bias can be tested against the composition of the other typologies of SC decisions adopted between 2001 and 2014, so long as resolutions represent only one quarter of all decisions taken.[1]

[1]Resolutions are generally regarded as the category of substantive SC decisions endowed with the greatest political importance. However, as the empirical data show, there is a tendency among scholars to focus only on resolutions. On the interpretation of SC resolutions, see Orakhelashvili (2007), p. 143, Wood (1998) and Yee (2012).

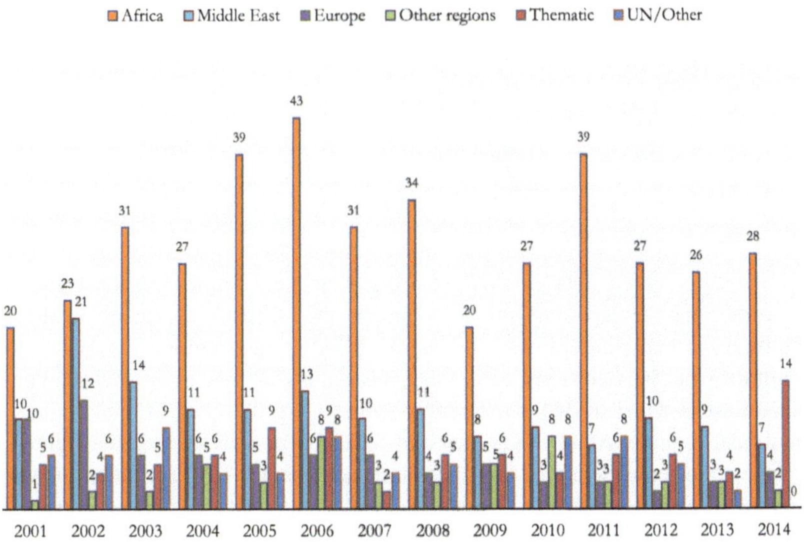

Fig. 5.4 Composition of resolutions (2001–2014)

Fig. 5.5 Aggregated data on composition of resolutions (2001–2014)

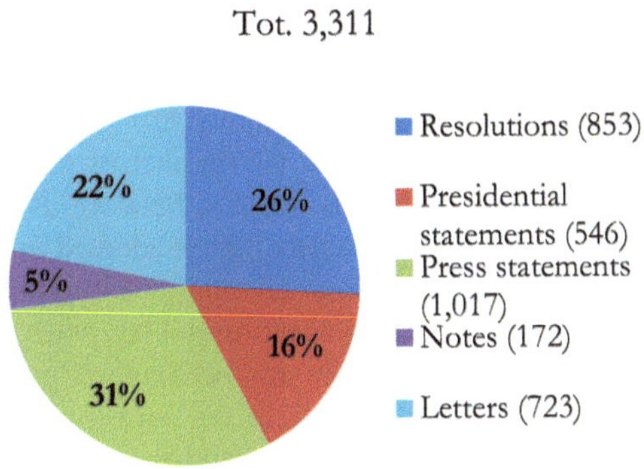

The disaggregated data on the entire spectrum of SC practice (2001–2014) show that the vast majority of decisions address issues on geopolitical regions, though in a significantly lower percentage compared to geopolitical resolutions (see Figs. 5.5 and 5.6). However, Table 5.4 shows that 58 % of decisions on country-specific or regional issues address situations taking place in Africa and the Middle East. The number nearly perfectly matches the percentage of resolutions adopted in the same period of time on the same subject-matter and this in turn suggests that the decisions adopted by the SC between 2001 and 2014 are tainted by selection bias.

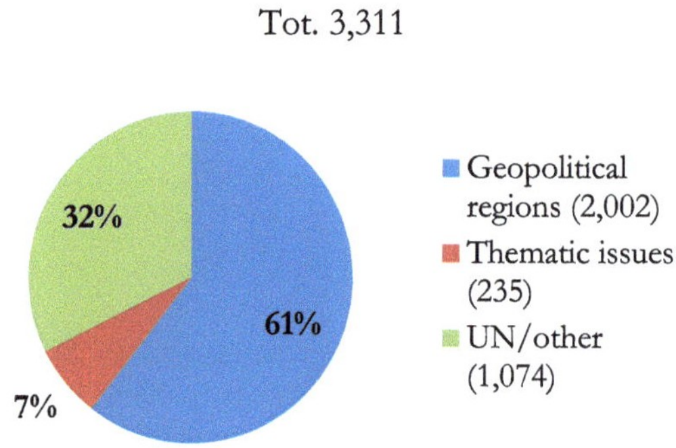

Fig. 5.6 Categories of resolutions (2001–2014)

Table 5.4 Disaggregated data on composition of decisions on geopolitical regions (2001–2014)

Geopolitical region	No. of decisions
Africa	1160 (58 %)
Middle East	557 (28 %)
Europe	147 (7 %)
Other regions	138 (7 %)
Total	2002 (100 %)

5.6 Assessing Selection Bias

Following on the previous analysis, it is significant that of the 1,715 resolutions on geopolitical regions adopted between 1946 and 2014, 743 resolutions—comprising 43 % of resolutions, address situations in Africa while 469 resolutions—comprising 27 % of resolutions, concern the Middle East region. Taken together, the number of resolutions on Africa and the Middle East is equal to 1,212, comprising 70 % of resolutions (see Table 5.5). Assuming that the SC has not acted *ultra vires*,[2] the findings of the empirical analysis also suggest that the actions taken by the SC address situations represent threats to international peace and security, and, therefore, fall under the purview of its mandate.

However, the major point of concern is that the margin of discretion in the hands of SC members in general, and the five permanent members (P5) in particular, reflects the scenario of international relations and diplomatic interactions between members of the international community.[3] Hence, the fact that such a huge number of resolutions targets situations in Africa and the Middle East suggests that the actions taken by the SC from 1946 to 2014, and especially during the twenty-first century, are tainted by selection bias.

[2]On this issue, see Rosand (2005).

[3]Steiner and Alston (2000), pp. 651–653 (discussing gross violations of human rights and the SC's impasse caused by political convenience of the P5). See also Smith (2010), p. 54 (arguing that '[t]he most serious compliant raised against the Security Council is that it is less likely to take action against its permanent members').

Table 5.5 Disaggregated data on composition of decisions on geopolitical regions (1946–2014)

Geopolitical region	No. of resolutions
Africa	743 (43%)
Middle East	469 (27%)
Europe	321 (19%)
Other regions	182 (11%)
Total	1715 (100%)

It is also true that a great number of SC resolutions refer to various types of international legal instruments, which include multiple references to general international law as well as international humanitarian, human rights and refugee law. Instruments of international law are endowed with a certain degree of objectivity, since they apply to the international community as a whole, subject to certain reservations to treaty law. In this respect, the empirical data shows that the resolutions on Africa contain a high number of generic references to international law—comprising general international law (214), international human rights law (194), international humanitarian law (430) and refugee law (36)—whereas resort to such generic references in the resolutions on the Middle East is rather contained—comprising general international law (37), international human rights law (40), international humanitarian law (88) and refugee law (4). Remarkably, the set of resolutions on the Democratic Republic of the Congo alone contains 125 references to international humanitarian law.

With the exception of the number of references to general international law, not even the thematic resolutions contain such a level of internationalization as the resolutions on Africa.[4] This shows that the same group of resolutions which appears to be tainted by selection bias is the one with the major concentration of references to international law. This in turn suggests that international law does not have a significant impact on SC practice nor it contributes the development of international law, with the exception of the field of international terrorism.[5] As a result, resort to international law is not able to contain the discretionary exercise of SC powers, but it rather appears to be a strong ground of justification for perpetuating the selection bias, which ultimately rests on the unquestionability of SC actions.

5.7 Reuniting 'Is' and 'Ought' in Security Council Practice

Overall, the numerical evidence yielded by this study shows that although individual SC decisions comply with the terms of its mandate, the selection of subject-matters representing the object of the decisions adopted between 1946 and

[4]The data for the thematic resolutions is as follows: international law (164), international human rights law (45), international humanitarian law (77) and refugee law (36).

[5]As discussed in Chap. 4, Sect. 4.3.4.

2014 ultimately amounts to a biased compliance with the UN Charter obligations. Perhaps, a possible remedy to turn this disproportionate amount of discretion in the hands of the SC permanent members into a more modest margin of appreciation would be to empower other principal bodies of the UN to oblige the SC to take into consideration the situations brought to his attention and to publicly justify its subsequent actions or inactions. From this perspective, the mandatory requirement that parties to an armed conflict ensure strict compliance with the relevant rules of humanitarian and human rights law as well as the UN Charter and SC resolutions[6] would be accepted as an objective benchmark of international legality. Moreover, this is not in contradiction with the SC's 'commitment to the Purposes of the Charter of the United Nations as set out in Article 1 of the Charter, and to the Principles of the Charter as set out in Article 2 thereof, including its commitment to the principles of the political independence, sovereign equality and territorial integrity of all States, and to respect for the sovereignty of all States.'[7]

As things stand, the SC has the power to decide the degree of necessity of its intervention based on political considerations.[8] Conversely, the reform of powers proposed above would shift the attention from a discretional parameter of global politics to an objective parameter of international legality. This would bring benefits for the international community as a whole, since international law does not discriminate on the basis of political convenience, and endow SC measures such as the one reported below with impartiality:

> The Security Council calls upon all parties concerned to comply strictly with their obligations under international law, in particular their relevant obligations under the Hague Conventions, the Geneva Conventions of 1949 and their Additional Protocols of 1977, and the United Nations Convention on the Rights of the Child of 1989, as well as with *all decisions of the Security Council.*[9]

However, as the numerical evidence yielded by this study shows, 70 % of issues of regional concern involve Africa and the Middle East and, within this figure, it turns out that there is a concentration of decisions in specific areas. Specifically, with regard to Africa, the majority of SC decisions address issues in the Democratic Republic of the Congo, Ivory Coast, Somalia and Sudan/South Sudan whereas considerably less attention is given to issues in areas such as the Great Lakes region and Libya. Furthermore, consideration of other areas characterized by political instability and popular unrest, such as Tunisia and Egypt, is absent. With regard to the Middle East, the vast majority of SC decisions address issues taking place in the

---

[6]Res. 1265(1999), paras. 3 and 4; Res. 1296(2000), Preamble, para. 7; PRST 2002/41, para. 3; PRST 2003/27, para. 2; PRST 2004/46, para. 3; and PRST 2010/25, para. 9.

[7]Res. 1296(2000), Preamble, para. 6; Res. 1674(2006), Preamble, para. 2; Res. 1738(2006), Preamble, para. 3; and Res. 1894(2009), Preamble, para. 2.

[8]In the Security Council resolutions and presidential statements on women, children and the protection of civilians in armed conflicts there are countless references to the unlimited discretion of the Security Council in assessing matters brought to its attentions ("where necessary" and "on a case-by-case basis"). See, for instance, PRST 2002/6, para. 3.

[9]PRST 1999/6, para. 6 (emphasis added).

Middle East region as a whole, and Afghanistan and Iraq in particular. Other areas such as Iran, Israel, Syria and Yemen are given marginal attention.

As a matter of fact, the coverage of issues—real or potential—threatening international peace and security by the SC is uneven. Since the SC can avail itself of an absolute discretion in the determination whether a threat to or breach of international peace and security under Chapter VII of the UN Charter exists,[10] serious doubts have been raised about the legitimacy of the actions and inactions of the SC.[11] Another approach to taming the SC powers may consist of an assessment of the implications of the empirical analysis on the internal and external coherence of current SC practice, with a view to reuniting what 'is' and what 'ought to be' current and future SC practice.[12]

The issue of external coherence refers to the relation between the SC and other UN organs—namely, the Secretary-General and the General Assembly. Previous studies have shown that because of the veto power, whether actual or threatened, certain decisions turn out to be impractical and have, therefore, suggested that alternative approaches and levels of discussion might help ameliorate the situation.[13] For instance, the level of decision-making regarding threats to or breaches of international peace and security could be shared with other primary organs of the UN, at least at the preliminary stages of discussion leading to the possible inclusion of a matter on the SC agenda.

One such organ is the Secretary-General. As established practice shows, there is an ongoing exchange of letters between the Secretary-General and the SC President on current and potential issues on the SC agenda.[14] However, although such an exchange is meant to improve the overall SC action strategy, the SC recognizes the role of the Secretary-General as merely consultative.[15] In strict legal terms, this restrictive attitude of the SC stems from the wording of the UN Charter by virtue of Article 24, which confers 'primary responsibility' on the SC for the maintenance of international peace and security. On the other side of the spectrum, Article 99 of the UN Charter may be invoked as the basis of the Secretary-General's political activities.[16] It reads:

> The Secretary-General may bring to the attention of the Security Council any matter which in his opinion may threaten the maintenance of international peace and security.

Although formulated in broad terms, the right of the Secretary-General under Article 99 has limited relevance in constraining the powers of the SC. As the history

---

[10]Gowlland-Debbas (1994), p. 662.

[11]Smith (2010), p. 54 (arguing that "[t]he most serious compliant raised against the Security Council is that it is less likely to take action against its permanent members").

[12]Fischman (2013), p. 168.

[13]Deplano (2014).

[14]Deplano (2014), pp. 148–149.

[15]Res. 1612(2005), para. 4; Res. 1882(2009), para. 2; Res. 1998(2011), para. 2; and PRST/2010/10, para. 16.

[16]Newman (2008), pp. 177–178.

of the drafting of Article 99 shows, the Secretary-General was not intended to preside over the SC or to dictate its agenda.[17] By no coincidence, the final formulation of Article 99 was proposed by a P5, thus confirming the political nature of the SC.[18]

Another alternative might consist of a duty of the SC to take into consideration matters referred to it by the General Assembly and publicly justify its decisions as to whether or not take action in light of applicable provisions of the UN Charter and international law. As things stand, the General Assembly may discuss any questions relating to the maintenance of international peace and security and make any recommendations to Member States and the SC on any such questions.[19] However, the rights of the General Assembly are subject to the provision of Article 12 of the UN Charter:

> While the Security Council is exercising in respect of any dispute or situation the functions assigned to it in the present Charter, the General Assembly shall not make any recommendation with regard to that dispute or situation unless the Security Council so requests.

Absent any duty of the SC to take into consideration situations of potential breach of international peace and security brought to its attention by other UN organs, such as the Secretary-General and the General Assembly, the possibility to create, and clarify, the normative parameter of legitimacy of SC actions is constantly jeopardized by the SC power to decide the degree of necessity of its intervention based on political considerations.[20] Given the broad formulation of Article 24 of the UN Charter, even the principle laid out by the ICJ on the political character of an organ of the UN, such as the SC, cannot be regarded as decisive in determining the legitimacy of SC actions:

> The political character of an organ cannot release it from the observance of the treaty provisions established by the Charter *when they constitute limitations on its powers or criteria for its judgment.* To ascertain whether an organ has *freedom of choice for its decisions*, reference must be made to the terms of its constitution.[21]

This has led certain international scholarship to conclude that 'such lack of accountability and failure to provide remedies against an injudicious Security Council in itself poses a threat to international peace and security.'[22]

Perhaps the best way to establish a benchmark of international legality would be to ensure a high level of internal coherence of SC decisions. Resolutions addressing

---

[17]Schwebel (1951), p. 371.

[18]Schwebel (1951), p. 374.

[19]UN Charter, Arts. 10–11.

[20]In the SC resolutions and presidential statements on women, children and civilians there are countless references to the unlimited discretion of the SC in assessing matters brought to its attentions ('where necessary' and 'on a case-by-case basis'). See, for instance, PRST/2002/6, para. 3.

[21]*Admission of a state to the United Nations (Charter, Article 4)* (Advisory Opinion) [1948] ICJ Rep. 57, at 64 (emphasis added).

[22]Rehman (2010), p. 39.

thematic issues, for example, could be used to set a parameter of legality for future SC actions. Such use of precedent would not be contrary to the SC mandate nor would it be perceived as an undue interference by the P5, since the content of thematic resolutions is decided by the SC itself. Conversely, it would bring benefit in the international legal system as it would start a process of codification of the legal mind of the SC. However, the effectiveness of this proposal is doubtful in many ways. In particular, whereas reasons of consistency and reasonableness of SC actions suggest that it is unlikely that the SC would treat identical situations in different ways without any serious justification, the definition of international peace and security is so broad that cannot eliminate selection bias relating to the issues included on the SC agenda.

5.8 Conclusion

This chapter has built a taxonomy of SC resolutions from 1946 to 2014. The findings of the analysis show that SC resolutions, especially those of the twenty-first century, are tainted by selection bias. However, actions taken so far by the SC fall within the purview of the SC mandate, as established in the UN Charter. The problem associated with the provisions of the UN Charter is that they confer a broad range of powers on the SC without providing a clear definition of international peace and security. This gives the SC a large margin of discretion in interpreting the maximum and minimum limits of its mandate without the need to justify its decisions before another UN body or international tribunal. Relying upon international law or international standards may be perceived as a welcome practice, as it fosters transparency in the SC decision-making process. However, as the empirical data shows, most of the resolutions in which the SC has invoked the provisions of international law are those charged of bias. The latter observation confirms that over the decades the SC has developed its own juridical mind.

Bibliography

Deplano, Rossana. 2014. Building a Taxonomy of UN Security Council Decisions: A Biased Compliance with the UN Charter Obligations?. *State Practice and International Law Journal* 1: 139–160.

Fischman, Joshua B. 2013. Reuniting 'Is' and 'Ought' in empirical legal scholarship. *University of Pennsylvania Law Review* 162: 117–168.

Gowlland-Debbas, Vera. 1994. The relationship between the international court of justice and the security council in light of the Lockerbie case. *American Journal of International Law* 88: 643–677.

Newman, Edward. 2008. In *The Oxford handbook on the United Nations*, eds. Thomas G. Weiss and Sam Daws, 175–192. New York: Oxford University Press.

Orakhelashvili, Alexander. 2007. The acts of the security council: meaning and standards of review. *Max Planck Yearbook of United Nations Law* 11: 143–195.

Rehman, Javaid. 2010. *International human rights law*. Harlow: Pearson Education Limited.
Rosand, Eric. 2005. The security council as "Global legislator": ultra vires or ultra innovative? *Fordham International Law Journal* 28: 542–590.
Schwebel, Stephen M. 1951. The origins and development of article 99 of the charter. *British Yearbook of International Law* 28: 371–382.
Smith, Rhona. 2010. *Textbook on international human rights*. Oxford: Oxford University Press.
Steiner, Henry J., and Philip Alston. 2000. *International human rights in context: law, politics, morals*. New York: Oxford University Press.
Wood, Michael C. 1998. The Interpretation of Security Council Resolutions. *Max Planck Yearbook of United Nations Law* 2: 73–95.
Yee, Sienho. 2012. The Dynamic Interplay between the Interpreters of Security Council Resolutions. *Chinese Journal of International Law* 11: 613–622.

Chapter 6
The Future Ahead

This study has presented the major findings of the first empirical analysis of seven decades of SC practice. It has outlined the normative background of the SC mandate and introduced an original, custom-built database on the use of international materials by the SC. The empirical data has been utilised as the basis for assessing certain profiles of SC practice against existent theoretical frameworks, which are often based on assumptions, with a view to complementing existent scholarly work on the SC powers from a different perspective.

The results of the study have significant practical implications. The key implication is that, as a political actor, the SC has the power to determine the course of international relations while, as a principal organ of the United Nations, it is legally bound by the provisions of the UN Charter and international law. However, there is an inherent tension between compliance with the terms of its mandate and a degree of discretion related to the selection of the subject matter of resolutions which seems unavoidable, especially in the absence of a well-defined definition of international peace and security.

Whatever the concept of international peace and security embraced by the SC, the task of maintaining international peace and security can be understood, broadly speaking, as a manifold act of dialogue among sovereign states and international institutions. Drawing from this assumption, this study has provided some numbers, which reconstruct, for the first time, the areas of concentration of SC resolutions.

The findings of the analysis show that the SC has developed a self-contained legal mind under the aegis of the UN Charter. Chap. 3, in particular, has demonstrated that references to primary sources of international law in the text of resolutions abound, and they seem to have some influence on the behavioral patterns of the SC. However, as the adopted resolutions do not set a precedent, the sources of international law cited therein fail to establish an objective parameter of international legality. In addition, Chap. 5 has shown that the resolutions of the SC, especially those adopted in the twenty-first century, are heavily characterized by selection preferences as to the subject matter, which ultimately amounts to a biased compliance with its UN Charter obligations.

This leads to the conclusion that while the discretionary powers of the SC cannot be eliminated, its commitment to enhancing existent regimes of international law such as human rights and humanitarian law exercises some influence over its

R. Deplano, *The Strategic Use of International Law by the United Nations Security Council*, SpringerBriefs in Law, DOI 10.1007/978-3-319-21281-4_6

politics, as the case of the resolutions on women, children, and civilians demonstrate. At the same time, this constructive attitude of the SC contributes to strengthening the authority of existent rules and principles of international law. On the other side of the spectrum, it appears that, outside the area of international terrorism, the scrutinized behavioral regularities of the SC have little or no influence on the development of international law.

As stated in Chap. 4, the SC resolutions on human rights issues have led to the crystallization of certain universally recognized human rights and set the scene for its own future activity, which is to be considered as characterised by a range of human rights constraints. Such constraints are expressions of what has been called 'self-imposed duties'—namely, duties that the SC has taken upon itself based on international law and a broad interpretation of the letter of the UN Charter. It is certainly a welcome development to see the SC exercising its powers in matters that are not specifically included in Chapter VII of the UN Charter. Therefore, the message that comes with the thematic resolutions analysed in this study is clear: human rights and humanitarian law violations constitute threats to international peace and security, and the SC should treat them as such.

However, the very foundations of these self-imposed duties being international law bring a few consequences that need to be underscored. The SC has traditionally been selective in the exercise of such duties, acting in some situations and ignoring others or refusing to intervene. Whether the reasons are to be found in the collective politics or in the internal dynamics of the SC is a matter for further research. What is relevant here is to underscore that human rights and humanitarian violations are to be considered as threats to the peace, breaches of the peace or acts of aggression under Chapter VII of the UN Charter. Consequently, the SC cannot afford to be selective and must exercise its powers in any situation that falls within the scope of its self-imposed duties.

Although the study of the legal implications of selection bias effects goes beyond the scope of the empirical treatment of this important legal phenomenon, further research could examine the political and legal significance of the systematic and prolonged intervention of the SC in two specific geopolitical regions—namely, Africa and the Middle East—and how the international community as a whole benefits from that, as well as the impact of the SC politics on the development of international law.

Appendix

(A) Resolutions of the origins and cold war period (1946–1991)

Subject	No. of Res.	Category	Sub-category
Admission of new members	100	UN/Other	–
Adolf Eichman case (question relating to)	1	UN/Other	–
Afghanistan-Pakistan	2	Geopolitical regions	Middle East
Angola	4	Geopolitical regions	Africa
Angola-South Africa	13	Geopolitical regions	Africa
Appointment of the UN Secretary-General	8	UN/Other	–
Arabic language in Security Council	1	UN/Other	–
Armaments: regulation and reduction	6	Thematic issue	–
Atomic energy: international control	3	Thematic issue	–
Bahrein (Question of)	1	Geopolitical regions	Middle East
Benin	3	Geopolitical regions	Africa
Botswana-South Africa	2	Geopolitical regions	Africa
Botswana-Southern Rhodesia	2	Geopolitical regions	Africa
Cambodia	4	Geopolitical regions	Other regions
Central America	9	Geopolitical regions	Other regions
Chad	1	Geopolitical regions	Africa
Chinese language in Security Council	1	UN/Other	–
Corfu Channel incidents	2	UN/Other	–
Cuba (compliant by)	1	Geopolitical regions	Other regions
Cyprus	82	Geopolitical regions	Europe
Democratic Republic of the Congo	10	Geopolitical regions	Africa

(continued)

R. Deplano, *The Strategic Use of International Law by the United Nations Security Council*, SpringerBriefs in Law, DOI 10.1007/978-3-319-21281-4

Subject	No. of Res.	Category	Sub-category
Dominican Republic (Question relating to)	3	Geopolitical regions	Other regions
East Timor	2	Geopolitical regions	Other regions
Egypt (compliant by)	2	Geopolitical regions	Africa
Egypt and Israel (Cease-fire between)	9	Geopolitical regions	Middle East
El Salvador	2	Geopolitical regions	Other regions
Falkland Islands (Malvinas)	2	Geopolitical regions	Other regions
Greece-Turkey	1	Geopolitical regions	Europe
Greek question	6	Geopolitical regions	Europe
Guatemala (question submitted by)	1	Geopolitical regions	Other regions
Guinea	4	Geopolitical regions	Africa
Hijacking of commercial aircraft	1	UN/Other	–
Honduras-Nicaragua	1	Geopolitical regions	Other regions
Hostage taking	3	Thematic issue	–
Hungary	1	Geopolitical regions	Europe
International Court of Justice	21	UN/Other	–
India-Pakistan (question of)	18	Geopolitical regions	Other regions
Indonesian question	14	Geopolitical regions	Other regions
International peace and security	2	Thematic issue	–
Iran	4	Geopolitical regions	Middle East
Iran-USA	3	Geopolitical regions	Middle East
Iraq	6	Geopolitical regions	Middle East
Iraq-Iran	17	Geopolitical regions	Middle East
Iraq-Israel	1	Geopolitical regions	Middle East
Israel-Lebanon	44	Geopolitical regions	Middle East
Israel-Syria	37	Geopolitical regions	Middle East
Israel-Tunisia	2	Geopolitical regions	Middle East
Korea (Republic of)	6	Geopolitical regions	Other regions
Laos	1	Geopolitical regions	Other regions
Lebanon	9	Geopolitical regions	Middle East
Lebanon, Jordan (complaint by)	1	Geopolitical regions	Middle East
Lesotho-South Africa	5	Geopolitical regions	Africa
Marking of explosives	1	Thematic resolution	–
Middle East	29	Geopolitical regions	Middle East
Military Staff Committee	1	UN/Other	–
Mozambique-Southern Rhodesia	2	Geopolitical regions	Africa
Namibia	25	Geopolitical regions	Africa
Nicaragua-USA	1	Geopolitical regions	Other regions
Non-nuclear weapons states	1	Thematic issue	–

(continued)

Subject	No. of Res.	Category	Sub-category
Pacific Islands (trust territory)	1	Geopolitical regions	Other regions
Palestine	34	Geopolitical regions	Middle East
Peace and security in Latin America	1	Geopolitical regions	Other regions
Peace Conference in Middle East	1	UN/Other	–
Procedure	6	UN/Other	–
Relations between Great Powers	1	Thematic issue	–
Request of Panama	1	Geopolitical regions	Other regions
Request of the Organization of African Unity	1	UN/Other	–
Review of the UN Charter	1	UN/Other	–
Seychelles	2	Geopolitical regions	Africa
Senegal	6	Geopolitical regions	Africa
Situation between Iraq and Kuwait	18	Geopolitical regions	Middle East
Socialist Federal Republic of Yugoslavia	3	Geopolitical regions	Europe
South Africa	26	Geopolitical regions	Africa
South Africa-Zambia	2	Geopolitical regions	Africa
Southern Rhodesia	23	Geopolitical regions	Africa
Southern Rhodesia-Zambia	2	Geopolitical regions	Africa
Spanish question	3	Geopolitical regions	Europe
Taiwan (Formosa)	1	Geopolitical regions	Other regions
Territories occupied by Israel	19	Geopolitical regions	Middle East
Territories under Portuguese administration	5	Geopolitical regions	Other regions
Travelling expenses	1	UN/Other	–
Trieste (free territory of)	1	Geopolitical regions	Europe
Trusteeship of strategic areas	2	UN/Other	–
Tunisia (complaint by)	1	Geopolitical regions	Africa
UN Emergency Force (UNEF)	1	UN/Other	–
UNEF for Middle East	1	UN/Other	–
West Africa	2	Geopolitical regions	Africa
Western Sahara	7	Geopolitical regions	Africa
Working languages of the Security Council	1	UN/Other	–
Yemen	2	Geopolitical regions	Middle East
Zambia (compliant by)	2	Geopolitical regions	Africa
Zambia's decision to impose sanctions	2	Geopolitical regions	Africa
Total	725		

(B) Resolutions of the post-cold war period (1992–2000)

Subject	No. of Res.	Category	Sub-category
Abkhazia	6	Geopolitical regions	Europe
Admission of new members	25	UN/Other	–
Afghanistan	5	Geopolitical regions	Middle East
Africa	3	Geopolitical regions	Africa
Africa, refugee camps	1	Geopolitical regions	Africa
Albania	2	Geopolitical regions	Europe
Angola	39	Geopolitical regions	Africa
Appointment of the UN Secretary-General	2	UN/Other	–
Armenia-Azerbaijan	4	Geopolitical regions	Middle East
Bosnia and Herzegovina	37	Geopolitical regions	Europe
Bosnia and Herzegovina and multilateral IFOR	1	Geopolitical regions	Europe
Burundi	4	Geopolitical regions	Africa
Cambodia	11	Geopolitical regions	Other regions
Central African Republic	9	Geopolitical regions	Africa
Central America: efforts towards peace	2	Geopolitical regions	Other regions
Children and armed conflict	2	Thematic issue	–
Closure of the border between the Federal Republic of Yugoslabia and Bosnia and Herzegovina	1	Geopolitical regions	Europe
Commission of experts (Rwanda)	1	Geopolitical regions	Africa
Croatia	22	Geopolitical regions	Europe
Croatia-Serbia	1	Geopolitical regions	Europe
Cyprus	23	Geopolitical regions	Europe
Democratic People's Republic of Korea	1	Geopolitical regions	Other regions
Democratic Republic of the Congo	9	Geopolitical regions	Africa
East Timor	4	Geopolitical regions	Other regions
Effective role for the Security Council in maintaining international peace and security, particularly in Africa	1	Thematic issue	–
El Salvador	5	Geopolitical regions	Other regions
Exemption from the provisions of Res. 747(1992)	1	Geopolitical regions	Europe
Exemption from the provisions of Res. 748(1992)	1	Geopolitical regions	Europe
Former Yugoslavia	15	Geopolitical regions	Europe

(continued)

Subject	No. of Res.	Category	Sub-category
Freedom of navigation on the Danube River	1	Geopolitical regions	Europe
Federal Republic of Yugoslavia	4	Geopolitical regions	Europe
Federal Republic of Yugoslavia (Serbia and Montenegro)	1	Geopolitical regions	Europe
Georgia	11	Geopolitical regions	Europe
Great Lakes Region	3	Geopolitical regions	Africa
Guinea-Bissau	2	Geopolitical regions	Africa
Haiti	17	Geopolitical regions	Other regions
HIV/AIDS and peacekeeping operations	1	Thematic issue	–
International Court of Justice (elections)	6	UN/Other	–
ICTR	8	UN/Other	–
ICTR and ICTY	2	UN/Other	–
ICTY	10	UN/Other	–
Illicit arms flow to and in Africa	1	Geopolitical regions	Africa
Implementation of the Report of the Panel on UN Peace Operations (S/2000/809)	1	Thematic issue	–
International Commission of Inquiry for the investigation of the arms flow to former Rwandan Government forces in the Great Lakes region	1	Geopolitical regions	Africa
International Commission of Inquiry in Burundi	1	Geopolitical regions	Africa
International peace and security	1	Thematic issue	–
International Police Task Force	1	Geopolitical regions	Europe
International terrorism	1	Thematic issue	–
Iraq	2	Geopolitical regions	Middle East
Israel-Lebanon	4	Geopolitical regions	Middle East
Israel-Syria	4	Geopolitical regions	Middle East
Kosovo	3	Geopolitical regions	Europe
Letter from the Permanent Representative of Ethiopia to the Security Council President (S/1996/10)	3	Geopolitical regions	Africa
Letters from the UK (S/1998/223) and the US (S/1998/272)	1	Geopolitical regions	Europe
Liberia	10	Geopolitical regions	Africa
Libya	3	Geopolitical regions	Africa
Lockerbie case	1	UN/Other	–

(continued)

Subject	No. of Res.	Category	Sub-category
Macedonia	11	Geopolitical regions	Europe
Middle East	21	Geopolitical regions	Middle East
Middle East, including the Palestinian question	1	Geopolitical regions	Middle East
Mozambique	3	Geopolitical regions	Africa
Occupied Arab Territories	1	Geopolitical regions	Middle East
Palau	1	Geopolitical regions	Other regions
Palestinian civilians	1	Geopolitical regions	Middle East
Protection of civilians in armed conflicts	2	Thematic issue	–
Resolutions 1160(1998), 1199 (1998) and 1203(1998)	1	Geopolitical regions	Europe
Responsibility of the Security Council in maintaining international peace and security	1	Thematic issue	–
Rwanda	9	Geopolitical regions	Africa
Sanctions against Yugoslavia	1	Geopolitical regions	Europe
Shooting down of two civil aircrafts on 24 February 1996	1	Thematic issue	–
Sierra Leone	18	Geopolitical regions	Africa
Situation between Eritrea and Ethiopia	7	Geopolitical regions	Africa
Situation between Iraq and Kuwait	29	Geopolitical regions	Middle East
Socialist Federal Republic of Yugoslavia	4	Geopolitical regions	Europe
Somalia	12	Geopolitical regions	Africa
South Africa	5	Geopolitical regions	Africa
Tajikistan	3	Geopolitical regions	Other regions
Tajikistan and Tajik-Afghan border	7	Geopolitical regions	Other regions
Territories occupied by Israel	2	Geopolitical regions	Middle East
Timor	3	Geopolitical regions	Other regions
UN Angola Verification Mission II-III	8	UN/Other	–
UN Aouzou Strip Observer Group	2	UN/Other	–
UN Assistance Mission for Rwanda	10	UN/Other	–
UN Confidence Restoration Mission in Croatia	4	UN/Other	–
UN Disengagement Observer Force	4	UN/Other	–
UN Interim Force in Lebanon	4	UN/Other	–

(continued)

Subject	No. of Res.	Category	Sub-category
UN Mission in Haiti	6	UN/Other	–
UN Mission of Observers in Liberia	7	UN/Other	–
UN Mission of Observers in Tajikistan	3	UN/Other	–
UN Observer Mission in El Salvador	3	UN/Other	–
UN Observer Mission in Georgia	6	UN/Other	–
UN Observer Mission in Uganda-Rwanda	1	UN/Other	–
UN Operation Mission in Mozambique	3	UN/Other	–
UN Operation in Somalia II	5	UN/Other	–
UN Peacekeeping: Dag Hammarskjöld Medal	1	UN/Other	–
UN Peacekeeping Force in Cyprus	4	UN/Other	–
UN peacekeeping operations	1	UN/Other	–
UN Preventive Deployment Force	2	UN/Other	–
UN Protection Force	8	UN/Other	–
Use of nuclear weapons	1	Thematic issue	–
Western Sahara	30	Geopolitical regions	Africa
Women and peace and security	1	Thematic issue	–
Yemen	2	Geopolitical regions	Middle East
Yugoslavia and Bosnia and Herzagovina	1	Geopolitical regions	Europe
Total	608		

(C) Resolutions of the twenty-first century period (2001–2014)

Subject	No. of Res.	Category	Sub-category
Admission of new members	4	UN/Other	–
Afghanistan	37	Geopolitical regions	Middle East
Angola	9	Geopolitical regions	Africa
Bosnia and Herzegovina	21	Geopolitical regions	Europe
Burundi	16	Geopolitical regions	Africa
Central African Republic	7	Geopolitical regions	Africa
Chad, Central African Republic and the subregion	6	Geopolitical regions	Africa
Children and armed conflict	8	Thematic issue	–
Cooperation between the UN and regional and subregional organizations in maintaining international peace and security	2	Thematic issue	–
Croatia	5	Geopolitical regions	Europe
Cyprus	28	Geopolitical regions	Europe
Date of election to fill a vacancy in the ICJ	5	UN/Other	–
Democratic Republic of the Congo	56	Geopolitical regions	Africa
East Timor	3	Geopolitical regions	Other regions
General issues relating to sanctions	3	Thematic issue	–
Georgia	18	Geopolitical regions	Europe
Great Lakes Region	2	Geopolitical regions	Africa
Guinea-Bissau	9	Geopolitical regions	Africa
Haiti	18	Geopolitical regions	Other regions
High-level meeting of the Security Council: Combating terrorism	1	Thematic issue	–
ICTR	24	UN/Other	–
ICTR and ICTY	4	UN/Other	–
ICTY	27	UN/Other	–
Iraq	19	Geopolitical regions	Middle East
Ivory Coast	53	Geopolitical regions	Africa
Kimberley process certification scheme	1	Geopolitical regions	Africa
Letters dated 1991 and 2003	1	UN/Other	–
Letters from the Permanent Representative of Japan (S/2006/481)	1	Geopolitical regions	Other regions
Letter from the Permanent Representative of Macedonia to the Security Council President (S/2001/191)	1	Geopolitical regions	Europe

(continued)

Subject	No. of Res.	Category	Sub-category
Letter from the Permanent Representative of Ukraine	1	Geopolitical regions	Europe
Letter from the Secretary-General (S/2006/920)	8	Geopolitical regions	Other regions
Liberia	44	Geopolitical regions	Africa
Libya	10	Geopolitical regions	Africa
Macedonia (The Former Yugoslav Republic of)	1	Geopolitical regions	Europe
Maintenance of international peace and security	2	Thematic issue	–
Maintenance of international peace and security: conflict prevention	1	Thematic issue	–
Maintenance of international peace and security: nuclear non-proliferation and nuclear disarmament	1	Thematic issue	–
Maintenance of international peace and security: security sector reform	1	Thematic issue	–
Mali	4	Geopolitical regions	Africa
Middle East	70	Geopolitical regions	Middle East
Middle East, including the Palestinian question	9	Geopolitical regions	Middle East
Non-proliferation	8	Thematic issue	–
Non-proliferation/Democratic People's Republic of Korea	8	Geopolitical regions	Other regions
Non-proliferation/Iran	2	Geopolitical regions	Middle East
Non-proliferation of weapons of mass destruction	5	Thematic issue	–
Peace and security in Africa	8	Geopolitical regions	Africa
Peace consolidation in West Africa	1	Geopolitical regions	Africa
Post-conflict peacebuilding	3	Thematic issue	–
Proliferation of small arms and light weapons (West Africa)	1	Geopolitical regions	Africa
Protection of civilians in armed conflicts	4	Thematic issue	–
Protection of UN and associate personnel	1	Thematic issue	–
Recommendations for the appointment of the Secretary-General	3	UN/Other	–
Reports of the Secretary-General on Sudan	28	Geopolitical regions	Africa

(continued)

Subject	No. of Res.	Category	Sub-category
Resolution 1054(1996)	1	Geopolitical regions	Africa
Resolution 1160(1998)	1	Geopolitical regions	Europe
Role of the Security Council in the prevention of armed conflicts	1	Thematic issue	–
Rwanda	2	Geopolitical regions	Africa
Security Council meetings in Nairobi	1	UN/Other	–
Sierra Leone	24	Geopolitical regions	Africa
Situation between Eritrea and Ethiopia	21	Geopolitical regions	Africa
Situation between Iraq and Kuwait	19	Geopolitical regions	Middle East
Small arms and light weapons	1	Thematic issue	–
Somalia	53	Geopolitical regions	Africa
Strengthening co-operation with troop contributing countries	1	UN/Other	–
Sudan	25	Geopolitical regions	Africa
Sudan sanctions	1	Geopolitical regions	Africa
Sudan/South Sudan	5	Geopolitical regions	Africa
Threats to international peace and security	2	Thematic issue	–
Threats to international peace and security (Security Council Summit 2005)	2	Thematic issue	–
Threats to international peace and security caused by terrorist acts	33	Thematic issue	–
Timor Leste	15	Geopolitical regions	Other regions
Tribute to the outgoing Secretary-General	1	UN/Other	–
UN peacekeeping operations	5	UN/Other	–
Western Sahara	28	Geopolitical regions	Africa
Women and peace and security	6	Thematic issue	–
Total	861		–

MIX
Papier aus verantwortungsvollen Quellen
Paper from responsible sources
FSC® C105338

If you have any concerns about our products,
you can contact us on
ProductSafety@springernature.com

In case Publisher is established outside the EU,
the EU authorized representative is:
Springer Nature Customer Service Center GmbH
Europaplatz 3, 69115 Heidelberg, Germany

Printed by Libri Plureos GmbH
in Hamburg, Germany